DATE		
	Jul 1 6 1991		

GRAHAM WATSON

THE TOUR DE FRANCE

and its heroes

A CELEBRATION OF
THE GREATEST RACE IN THE WORLD

STANLEY PAUL

London Sydney Auckland Johannesburg

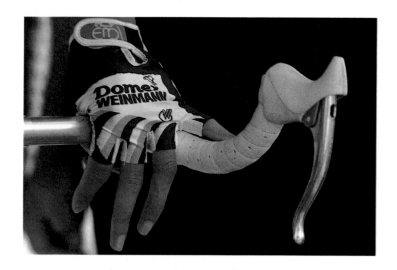

Previous pages: Race leader Stephen Roche and 'King of the Mountains' Luis Herrera descend through the greenery of the Savoie Alps

Stanley Paul & Co. Ltd

An imprint of Random Century Ltd

20 Vauxhall Bridge Road, London SW1V 2SA

Random Century Australia Pty Ltd
20 Alfred Street, Milsons Point, Sydney, NSW 2061

Random Century New Zealand Limited
191 Archers Road, PO Box 40–086, Glenfield, Auckland 10

Century Hutchinson South Africa (Pty) Ltd
PO Box 337, Bergvlei 2012, South Africa

First published 1990

Copyright © Graham Watson 1990

The right of Graham Watson to be identified as the author of this work has been asserted by him in accordance with the Copyright, Designs and Patents Act, 1988

Set in 10/14pt Frutiger 45 by TA Tek Art Ltd, Croydon, Surrey

Printed and bound in Italy by New Interlitho S.P.A.

British Library Cataloguing in Publication Data
    The Tour de France and its heroes: a celebration of the
    greatest race in the world
    1. France. Bicycles. Racing. Races: Tour de France, history
    1. Title
    796.620944

ISBN 0 09 174465 2

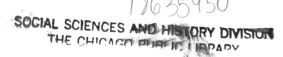

CONTENTS

Foreword   6

Introduction   8

The Hinault years   22

On a wing and a prayer   54

Heroes   82

Race for the Green Jersey   98

The 'New World' makes its entry   118

Laurent Fignon: unrestored glory   152

Into the 21st century   162

Tour facts   170

Index   175

FOREWORD

The Tour de France is incontestably the greatest cycle race in the world. Its impressive history and the tremendous interest generated by the media every year make it extremely attractive to the public. But above all, it is the heroic exploits seen in the race itself that excite the greatest passion. The public recognize the extraordinary valour of the winners, as well as the distress of cyclists who often finish the race with difficulty and in pain.

The objective of the photographer is to capture images of the courage of these 'heroes of modern times' who continually seek to push back the limits of what is achievable and what is then sufferable. Perched on a motorbike or enveloped by thousands of screaming roadside fans, the photographer is intimately linked to the cyclists' emotions . . . their moments of intense happiness or despair, and their anguish. In this case the photographer is also the author and Graham Watson has thus been able to convey a complete picture of the Tour. His book will enable you to live this grand adventure that is the Tour de France.

Eddy Merckx

Eddy Merckx, pictured here in 1977 during his last Tour de France, is acknowledged as the greatest ever cyclist. His stunning career record includes five Tour de France victories. He also won three world championships, five Tours of Italy, one Tour of Spain and a host of one-day classics such as seven Milan–San Remos, five Liège–Bastogne–Liège, three Paris–Roubaix and two Tours of Flanders. His self-stated career highlight was breaking the one-hour record in 1972 in Mexico City, where he covered 49·432 kilometres in 60 agonizing minutes

Eddy Merckx, a much-
celebrated figure within
the sport, is now a
highly successful cycle
manufacturer

INTRODUCTION

In 1904, a 32-year-old Frenchman, Maurice Garin, in company with five other cyclists, was climbing the Col de la République in the early hours of a July morning, having left the city of Lyon many hours earlier on this second stage of the second-ever Tour de France. Garin had won the inaugural Tour de France the previous year, and as the natural favourite this time around it was he who set the pace up the tree-lined climb, using the support cars' lights to guide him to the summit in the absence of any moon. Night riding was a feature of the Tour in its early years, a necessity brought about by the horrendously long stages like this one, that would take the fifty-odd survivors from the first leg – an 18-hour marathon – down the Rhône valley and beyond to the city of Marseille. It was not unusual to see throngs of spectators along the way even at three o'clock in the morning, for the inaugural Tour had captivated the public's imagination for this tough, new sporting challenge in an undreamed-of way. But when a group of about one hundred people started attacking the leading riders with clubs and stones at the summit of the République, it cast an altogether different light on the future prospects of this 'race around France' – as journalist Géo Lefèvre described the event.

All but one of the battered and bruised cyclists were eventually allowed to proceed on their way – the Italian Gerbi being too badly injured – but only after local hero Faure had passed through untouched, as the spectators loyal to this local St Etienne man had sought to hinder his rivals. It had been Lefèvre, travelling in one of the support cars, who had scared the attackers away by firing pistol shots into the night air. Ironically, Faure was overtaken by his chasers long before Marseille was reached, 300 kilometres down the road, but word spread of the hostility shown to the cyclists in the Tour through the pages of *L'Auto**, the newspaper that had organized the event. So, for the remainder of the six-stage race, the Tour and its competitors became the target of attacks or protests from other groups of rival supporters who had

Rugged mountain scenery, thousands of cheering fans, sunshine . . . the perfect image of the Tour de France

L'Auto changed its name to *L'Equipe* at the end of the Second World War.

taken note of the vulnerability of the cyclists during the long, dark nights.

Garin raced into Paris four stages later to cross the finish-line as winner for the second year in succession; but this was after worse trouble had befallen the race on that last stage from Nantes, with all kinds of obstacles being laid across the roads on the approach to the capital. At several points along the route, whole trees had been felled in an attempt to block various riders' progress – including Garin and his arch rival Pothier, whom the former managed to beat in a sprint in the Parc des Princes stadium. Such was the confusion over the whole result, that nobody could be too sure which, if any, of the leading riders had been in collusion with the roadside thugs. It was even suggested that some devious cyclists had accepted lifts in supporters' cars to leapfrog ahead of the race! Consequently, the first four riders on general classification, including Garin and his brother César, were disqualified for 'irregularities' in their racing. Despite his proclaimed innocence in the whole affair, Garin was suspended for two years, and chose never to race again in the Tour, while his rival Pothier was banished for life.

In only its second year, the Tour could hardly have met with a worse scandal, with its creator, Henri Desgrange sadly airing his doubts: 'The Tour is finished,' he wrote in his editorial the day after the disqualifications were announced. In such a short length of time, the race had generated so much interest around the country that avid sports fans became too emotionally involved, with the result that their passions had seemingly killed off the race. Fortunately, the Tour survived the débâcle of 1904, with some harsh lessons being learnt in the process, and returned the next year to become the most important cycle race of the year. At that time, cycling was the most popular sport on the Continental mainland, and the Tour de France was an extension of the increasingly popular formula of city-to-city races such as Paris–Roubaix, which now, at its 88th running, is the most sought-after one-day 'classic' to win. So, too, the Tour de France became the most prestigious of all races – it was certainly the toughest – to the extent that no

matter how many 'classics' or other national Tours a cyclist might win, he couldn't be considered amongst the true legends of cycling if he hadn't won at least one Tour de France. (The Vuelta à España and Giro d'Italia are the two most important stage-races to win after the French race.)

Since those early years, the Tour has survived a multitude of incidents, and was sufficiently well established to recommence after the First and the Second World Wars had interrupted its sequence. Nowadays student demonstrations, strikers' protests – even terrorist attacks – attempt to halt the race. But the Tour de France has proved itself a giant amongst national institutions, and as such has never really allowed itself to be seriously threatened. Fortunately the modern Tour still takes its lead from the 'Giants of the Road': men like Garin, who, having twice been a Paris–Roubaix winner, took his winner, took his already enviable career record into the first-ever Tour and laid the foundations for all those victorious men who emulated his courage and ability. Heroic as Garin's daunting efforts were, however, the stocky chimney-sweep will always have to share his renown with someone who, perhaps more than anybody else, personifies the immortal Tour de France hero. Eugène Christophe should have won two Tours but both times he suffered the most appalling misfortune whilst leading the race. The most recited incident occurred in 1913, when Christophe broke his front fork-stem on the treacherous descent of the Col du Tourmalet. The rules then forbade any outside assistance, and the race leader had

to carry his bike all the way down the unsurfaced path to
St Marie de Campan 12 kilometres away, where locals directed
him to a blacksmith's forge.

Under the scrutiny of officials, the exhausted cyclist
worked, unperturbed by the need to weld together his broken
frame with tools created only for repairing horse-irons; but he
then made the mistake of allowing a small boy to work the
bellows in order to keep the fire alight. It's difficult to imagine
in these days when sophisticated race service is available at a
moment's notice from a specially adapted car, the scene that
afternoon in the little forge in the Pyrenees. But Christophe's
public appeal was further reinforced when heartless officials –
headed by the tyrannical Desgrange – penalized him 3 minutes
for using the boy to help him. And that was in addition to the
two hours he'd lost effecting the repair. His 1919 loss – again
through a broken frame – was less romantic, yet equally
galling; for Christophe had been wearing the first ever *Yellow
Jersey*, a symbol of race leadership that was designed by
Desgrange to allow roadside spectators to know who was out
in front. Its colour just happened to be the same as the paper
on which *L'Auto* was printed.

The state of roads and equipment today may have eased
the pain and suffering immeasurably since the turn of the
century, but along the roads of the Tour de France there still
lie similar perils to those faced by the pioneers of the Tour like
Garin and Christophe. When Bernard Hinault crashed head first
onto the streets of St Etienne in 1985, his recovery and
subsequent overall victory was straight out of the legend
created by those early swashbuckling characters. Hinault's
achievements fall at the furthest end of the spectrum from
Garin. He is the last person to have won the Tour five times, a
record that only two other men share down the years. The
effect his stifling domination had on the Tour was such that
even now, five years after he last won, the Tour de France
peloton is still without a 'patron'. His iron-handed dictatorship
became almost as legendary as the deeds of Desgrange to
make the Tour what it still is today – the greatest annual
sporting event in the world.

While Hinault can identify with Garin, it's the men he's beaten in winning those Tours who provide the greatest interest. For the Tour de France is not just about winning – that's for the lucky few; more than anything else, it's about surviving. Cyclists do this in a variety of ways in the Tour. Some really do just survive, happy to reach Paris with no thoughts of winning anything more than the respect one's local community bestows on a Tour finisher, and the increased salary his reputation can realize. Between this category and the top men, there is spread out a veritable feast of talent, and for this reason, several competitions take place within the overall framework to cater for those men who know they will never win the Yellow Jersey outright. Of these inner races, the most difficult to win is the points competition, and to add increased importance to this most cut-throat of all the competitions, a *Green* Jersey was first awarded in 1953.

The Eiffel Tower and the Tour de France go together like good food and fine wine . . . . The survivors of the 1988 Tour cascade into the centre of Paris, their agonies forgotten and their celebrations about to begin

Sean Kelly's strongest asset is his iron-like constitution, much needed in the high mountains where so often the Tour de France has slipped away from him. Kelly is seen here in superb form approaching the summit of the feared Col d'Izoard during the 1989 Tour, just a few seconds behind the eventual Tour winner, Greg LeMond

Thirty-six years after its creation, Irishman Sean Kelly became the first person to win the points title four times, and like Hinault, his contribution to the legend of the Tour de France will only really be felt when he retires. Certainly, the men Kelly has shown his back wheel to on so many occasions will notice his absence, for the Irishman's influence on the Green Jersey competition is as strong as that which Hinault enforced on his own rivals. To win a Tour de France, one must possess a diversity of strengths and skills far superior to anything that most people can even relate to. At 34 years old Kelly never will win the Tour. In the prime of his career, during the early 1980s, Kelly was able to outspeed Tour winners in time-trials, and to outwit anybody in the packed sprints, as well as infiltrate any serious-looking breakaway group. Yet the one discipline that handicapped him was his climbing. If the Tour was only two weeks long, then for sure Kelly would have won at least one race in his eleven attempts, but always in the last week, on the highest and hardest climbs, the heat and fatigue penetrated even his leathery exterior.

Climbing is THE most enviable of all forms of cycle racing, and its romanticism is obvious, when one sees for the first time a group of cyclists inching their way up a 20-kilometre Col, dwarfed to the size of ants by their mighty surroundings. Not surprisingly it's also the most desired discipline, as an ability to ride free from pain in the thin air considerably enhances one's chances of success in the Tour.

Like the Green Jersey, a special category was designed for the 'mountain-goat' climber, and this competition is as much sought after – though not as tough – as the race for the Green Jersey. Because both the Yellow, and the *Polka-dot* Jerseys are competed for in the mountains, there's increased media interest when the Tour arrives at the foothills of the Pyrenees and Alps. The way in which tales of daring and courage filter back to the outside world is itself part of the suspense-building drama that sets the Tour apart from other sporting events, and the way in which this happens has changed a lot since the first time mountains were included in the Tour's itinerary in 1910.

With its polka-dots the leading climber's jersey is certainly eye-catching. Holland's Steven Rooks at the summit of Guzet-Neige in the 1988 Tour

The modern Tour has come a long way since the days when just a small handful of newsmen reported the race. Here, a motorbike-mounted television cameraman hovers next to Luis Herrera as the Colombian takes off in the mountains during the 1987 Tour. It's estimated that up to one billion people watch the Tour de France on television each year thanks to the use of space-age communications . . .

... and the skill of acrobatic cameramen

Desgrange, forever seeking maximum publicity for his race, built up rumours that the mountains these cyclists would have to pedal up in the Pyrenees were overrun by wild bears. On the 5,590 foot (1,704 metre) Col d'Aubisque, Desgrange had arranged for a car full of journalists to be waiting at the summit of this atrocious climb to record the reactions of the first cyclists to arrive. After an interminable wait, two insignificant figures were spotted down the mountain, both of them walking their bicycles up the narrow track. The second figure was Octave Lapize, who was to go on and win this Tour. Asked for his comments at the summit, all Lapize could manage to gasp was 'Murderers! Murderers!'. The astounded journalists scurried back to their car to speed off to the finish in Bayonne, where later, Desgrange permitted himself a wry smile – the headlines Lapize's words were to create in the newspapers a few days hence would only attract further interest in his race!

Nowadays, an array of modern communication systems allows up-to-date news of the race to be transmitted anywhere in the world instantly. If Desgrange were alive today, and had waited on the Aubisque summit when the Tour crossed over in 1989, he'd have seen not one car, but thousands – literally – including dozens of press-carrying cars and motorbikes actually moving with the riders. Additionally, he'd have seen at least two television helicopters, one mobile editing studio complete with satellite dish, as well as two specially adapted cars belonging to Colombia's radio network, their telescopic antennae sending live commentary to Bogotá, despite the fact that it would be the middle of the night there! This vast media presence reflects the truly international flavour the Tour de France enjoys at the end of the twentieth century. No longer is it just a race for a few hardy French, Belgian or Italian cyclists – now, cyclists from as far off as the United States and Australia line up with Colombians and Scandinavians. Even a Soviet team is rumoured to be entering in 1990.

The last decade has seen the most significant changes in the Tour in all its seventy-six turbulent yet triumphant years. Instead of just French winners, we've seen an Irishman and a

Bernard Hinault was a formidable opponent in the eight Tours de France he rode in. His spirit and attitude to racing were very much in the style of his predecessors Jacques Anquetil and Eddy Merckx, yet as the mid-1980s approached, Hinault adopted a more sophisticated, even scientific approach in order to stay on top. Here he is aided by ultra-modern equipment in the 1986 Prologue time-trial

1986: his clenched fist raised in triumph, Greg LeMond acknowledges the cheers of the crowds on the Champs Elysées, very aware of the enormity of his achievement in becoming the first non-European to win the Tour

Spaniard too, but most importantly as far as the worldwide appeal of the Tour goes, an American – Greg LeMond – has won twice. That he defeated two cycling colossi for good measure only adds to the magnitude of his achievements. In the *Tour de France and Its Heroes*, much has been made of the exploits of one of the men LeMond beat – Bernard Hinault – and with good reason, for every once in a while the Tour needs someone like Hinault to group the years together. An added significance is that Hinault's reign acts as a distinct link between the old-style Tours and the sophistication of a modern one. Casting an eye back through the history of the race, one's glance rests on similar giants: Lucien Petit-Breton, the first man to win two successive Tours in 1907 and 1908, and who might have won more if the First World War hadn't taken his life; Italy's first – and still foremost – *campionissimo*, Fausto Coppi, who had to wait till the Second World War had ended before he twice won the Tour, and whose tardy reign was terminated by Louison Bobet in 1953.

Bobet came from Brittany, and the tales of his three successive Tour victories were a significant inspiration in the childhood days of another young Breton – Bernard Hinault. But Hinault was just two years old, when Jacques Anquetil – a cyclist from the rival Normandy region of the country – won the first of his record-breaking five victories. Anquetil, Eddy Merckx – the next five-times winner – and Hinault are the absolute Almighties of Tour de France fable. Whether LeMond joins these three in the mid-1990s as a quintuple winner remains to be seen. But the significance of his 1986 victory, the subsequent shooting accident that almost cost him his life, and the herculean efforts he made to regain his crown in 1989, mean that the title of this book could well have been created just for LeMond, for he really is the latest, and potentially most glorious, Tour de France hero.

THE HINAULT YEARS

He's been called stubborn, arrogant, autocratic, egotistical –
even rebellious. His nickname is 'The Badger'. His actual name
is Bernard Hinault. Between 1978 and 1986 he won the Tour
de France five times, equalling a record set by only two men
before – France's Jacques Anquetil and Belgium's Eddy Merckx.
In the process Hinault dominated the minds and bodies of all
the cyclists competing in those same Tours in a different way
from Anquetil or Merckx, by instilling in them his own brand of
discipline and giving vent to a fiercely burning pride that
manifested itself in the most impressive way possible – by
means of his legs. The man was completely indefatigable in the
way he went about his business of winning the Tour,
apparently with records or statistics meaning little to him. For
Hinault, the only thing that mattered was showing everybody
just how unbeatable he was. That he did this for the most part
by leading from the front, made him all the more formidable
an opponent.

Hinault's domineering style of leadership was never likely
to win him many friends, but then that in itself probably never
bothered him, for the man was a law unto himself, dictating
not only how the Tour would be raced each and every day, but
also to what degree his rivals would be 'allowed' to participate
in his one-man show. For that's what the Tour de France
became in the late 1970s and early 1980s with Hinault: a one-
man exhibition on how to intimidate – and then annihilate –
the best cyclists in the world.

1978

The 23-year-old Hinault entered the Tour de France scene at a
time when French cycling was already on a 'high', following
two recent victories of the great race by Bernard Thevenet – in
1975 and 1977. But more significant was the sense of
anticipation felt by the French at Hinault's début, for the
country had been thirsting for this moment since the young
Breton turned professional in 1975, after a very short, yet
illustrious amateur career. 'This Hinault,' the country was told
by the media, 'he'll be as good as Merckx one day.' And that's
just what Hinault set out to be. Eddy Merckx at that time was

This photograph,
perhaps more than any
other, displays the full
might of Hinault's
devastating time-
trialling power.
Strength, determination
and concentration – all
played a huge part in
Hinault's eight-year
domination of the Tour
de France

Wearing his Champion of France jersey, Bernard Hinault clinched his first Tour victory in the last time-trial stage of the 1978 race

considered to be the best cyclist the world had ever seen – in fact would ever see. When Hinault became a professional, Merckx's career had just started to level off, and it was he whom Thevenet defeated to win the 1975 Tour. By the time Hinault took his place on the start-line at Leiden in Holland for the opening stage of the 1978 Tour, Merckx was no longer a professional cyclist, having retired earlier that spring. His absence from the Tour caused almost as much publicity as Hinault's long-awaited attendance. By the time Hinault rolled into Paris as the race winner 23 days later, the world knew Merckx's successor had already been found.

In many ways his first Tour de France was Hinault's hardest, largely because he was entering unknown territory, and his reaction to it was being scrutinized by half of France, if not Europe. Once he'd got that first win under his belt, Hinault never looked back, and perhaps he regretted having taken a comparatively timid approach to the 1978 race. He ultimately won it in the way he said he would – by staying close to the lead all the way through, but leaving his winning effort until the crucial time-trial between Metz and Nancy. Hinault's acknowledged speciality at that time was his ability against the clock, and thirteen days earlier he had convincingly won the only other time-trial in the race. Now, on the 75-kilometre road to Nancy, he duly trounced the race leader Joop Zoetemelk to take his first ever Yellow Jersey, a deed that allowed him to ride onto the Champs Elysées two days later as winner of the 1978 Tour de France. That then was the bare script for Hinault's winning début, though things might have been very different for him, and possibly for cycling in general, had it not been for an incident at L'Alpe d'Huez in the last week.

Michel Pollentier, an ungainly-looking Belgian and, at the time, his country's national champion, had established himself as the only serious threat to Hinault during the fortnight leading up to the Alpe d'Huez stage, being just 48 seconds behind Hinault on overall time when the riders set out that morning from St Etienne. By the time he'd attacked alone on the penultimate Col de Luitel and taken his stage lead to over two minutes as he began to climb L'Alpe d'Huez, Pollentier

25

was race leader 'on the road'. By the time he'd won the stage, he still had enough advantage, despite Hinault's desperate chase, to don the Yellow Jersey and present the Breton and his expectant public with a serious problem. Could their favourite actually be beaten by this little Belgian wondered some anxious French journalists.

They were never to find an answer. Scarcely had they sat down for dinner later that evening, when an announcement was issued to the Press that Pollentier had been expelled from the race for trying to cheat the drug control. It was alleged that he had substituted someone else's urine for his own as the test was being taken, something the 27-year-old didn't deny. Before the banished ex-leader left next morning for his native country he expressed sadness at the blight this incident had cast on him, on the hallowed Yellow Jersey, and on the sport itself. What he didn't say, though some of his team-mates and countrymen said it for him, was that he was being made a scapegoat to suit the organizers' interests vis-à-vis a Hinault victory; certain French riders, picked at random for the same dope-control that day, had apparently attempted the same trick – but had surprisingly been exonerated from blame.

Some speculators even went so far as to suggest that the organizers had paid for Pollentier's rather curious silence over the whole affair. Whether there was any truth in this will probably never be known, but it's interesting to speculate now, more than a decade later, whether Pollentier might have beaten Hinault that year: as winner of the previous year's Tour of Italy, he had all the right qualities to do so. If he had, it might have changed the direction of both men's careers. Hinault's career grew to legendary proportions, cultivating a massive industry in France in particular – Pollentier didn't finish the next two Tours de France he entered, and he eventually retired altogether in 1984 without achieving his full potential.

1979

Hinault's next victory in the Tour carried little in the way of scandal, but was rather a continuing saga of his all-conquering domination. In 1979 only Zoetemelk – again – could provide a

Joaquim Agostinho finished third overall for the second year running in 1979, a superb achievement for a 36 year old and one that saw him overtake a string of far younger men as the race reached its toughest section in the French Alps. Agostinho is pictured here at the mountain time-trial from Evian to Avoriaz, just a few days before his finest ever performance – a stage win at L'Alpe d'Huez. Sadly, this likeable Portuguese cyclist was killed in a minor stage race in Portugal, when a stray dog ran into his path in a bunch-sprint

challenge to Hinault, as a proliferation of time-trials and a dearth of tough mountain stages enabled Hinault to dictate too easily. On only one occasion did Hinault slip up, on the cobbled roads that led to Roubaix on stage 9. And it was Zoetemelk who gained time – and temporarily took Hinault's Yellow Jersey – as the Frenchman suffered a succession of punctures on the bad roads. Such was their personal battle that by the time the race entered the Alps with eleven days still to go, Dutchman Hennie Kuiper, the third-placed rider, was already twelve minutes in arrears!

Fittingly, though nobody could understand just how they were allowed to succeed, Hinault and his rival took off towards the end of the final stage, and rode almost ceremoniously around the Champs Elysées circuit in front of an ecstatic audience. Hinault's final winning margin over Zoetemelk was barely 3 minutes – but over Portugal's Joaquim Agostinho, now in third place, it had grown to an amazing 26½ minutes.

1980

1980 seemed to be heading the same way as the previous two years for the double Tour de France winner. Arriving fresh from a relatively comfortable win in the Tour of Italy, Hinault made his intention clear to all by taking his first-ever Tour de France Prologue win in Frankfurt. (The West German city paid an estimated $500,000 to stage the opening section of the Tour.) The stocky Breton, with the added confidence of having a particularly strong Renault-Gitane team behind him, was then content to let others fight for the Yellow Jersey as the race turned towards its mother country, for Hinault knew he had two medium-distance time-trials in the coming ten days in which to enforce his position. And that he duly did, riding into the Yellow Jersey two days before the tough Pyrenees stages. But that's as far as he got.

For the second year in a row, the cobbles of northern France inflicted their damage on the Frenchman. Though he won the sixth stage into Lille, beating Hennie Kuiper in a two-man sprint, his right knee began to show signs of wear and tear in the cold, rainy conditions. He may have pulverized the opposition on those slippery, bone-shaking cobbles, but next day Hinault began to look human after all, as repeated visits to the doctor's car became the order of the day. He rode through the next five days as delicately as possible, and despite soft-pedalling in the longest time-trial in the race to Laplume, still became race leader once again. But next evening, on the eve of perhaps the toughest stage in the Tour, Hinault visited the race organizers to break the news that he was going home that night – his tendonitis-damaged knee could take no more.

And so the increasingly rampant march of Bernard Hinault had been halted, albeit by an unseen force, and the 1980 Tour de France had a new leader in 33-year-old Joop Zoetemelk, though overnight the race had become a bit like the *Marie Celeste* – a floating ship with no sign of life. There was no question that had Hinault been there he would have won, but there was some consolation in seeing Zoetemelk finally pull off a Tour victory, for there aren't many cyclists with his potential whose careers have had the misfortune to clash with those of

Hinault's withdrawal halfway through the 1980 race left Joop Zoetemelk as race leader. Here, the Dutchman stretches the legs of third-placed Raymond Martin, second-placed Hennie Kuiper, and former Tour winner Lucien Van Impe on a stage to St Etienne. Had Van Impe been in better physical shape, the little Belgian could have provided Zoetemelk with his only serious challenge in what proved to be a rather lackadaisical race

Merckx *and* Hinault! And Zoetemelk – riding a British-made Raleigh bike – was honest enough to acknowledge his gratuity. He expected, like everybody else, that next year Hinault would be back with a vengeance. What nobody could have foreseen then, was the difference one year could make.

1981 and 1982

It was a stronger, wiser, more determined Hinault who took his place on the start-line of the 1981 Tour de France in Nice, having won the previous day's Prologue time-trial on the Promenade des Anglais at a staggering 54 kilometres per hour. Barely six weeks after abandoning the previous year's race, Hinault had matter-of-factly destroyed the opposition to become World Champion in the French town of Sallanches. It's worth mentioning this fact here, because that world's victory was achieved on a foundation of a crippling knee injury, and against some severe criticism from the European press. In retiring from the Tour in 1980, Hinault had found himself subjected to rumours that his knee injury had been caused through overuse of cortisone – a muscle-strengthening steroid that it was of course illegal to take. Additionally, the French press had criticized Hinault for the sudden way in which he'd taken his leave from the race – without giving them a chance to cross-examine him. In all Hinault's racing years, there was not one victory that saw him as motivated as he was in Sallanches. It was, by his own admission, 'the greatest day in my life', and the most exacting response to criticism anyone could have produced.

That Hinault continued his winning ways in the 1981 and 1982 Tours de France is now history. As is the fact that, in 1981, he won it by the biggest margin since Merckx's 1969 Tour debut – 14½ minutes – and at what was then a record average speed for any Tour de France – almost 38 kilometres per hour. What is significant is that Hinault's third Tour victory in 1981 represented a new phase in his career, one that would see a marked change in the man's character. For that six-week period of failure and success in 1980 had ignited a spark deep within him, and the fire would continue to burn till the end of

Showing what a difference adequate preparation can make, Van Impe gave Hinault a hard time on more than one occasion during the 1981 Tour – but still finished more than fourteen minutes behind the Frenchman in second place. Van Impe leads Hinault over the Col de Cou shortly before the 17th-stage finish in Thonon-les-Bains

The 1981 Tour gave Hinault's time-trialling skills a more than adequate showing, and helped him coast towards his biggest ever overall advantage. The Breton is seen here winning the Saint Priest test with two days to go before Paris, adding another 2:26 to his lead over Van Impe

Phil Anderson donned the Yellow Jersey in his very first Tour (1981) and shook Hinault's confidence in the process by dropping him at the summit finish of a tough Pyrenean stage. The Australian is seen here in all his athletic glory unsuccessfully defending his overall lead in the short 7th-stage time-trial to Pau

his career. Accordingly, it made Hinault an even more indomitable opponent, one who could mesmerize any would-be challengers with a display of strength, and if necessary, a teasing psychology. Perhaps that's why, with the exception of an Australian newcomer, Phil Anderson, who startled the race favourite with some aggressive riding, few riders did think of challenging for Hinault's crown in 1981 and 1982.

An extremely worthy successor to Hinault was found during the Breton's absence due to injury in the 1983 Tour – team-mate Laurent Fignon. The bespectacled Parisian, seen here during the mountain time-trial to Avoriaz in the Alps, went on to win the event the following year too – equalling all of Hinault's acknowledged skills in time-trialling and exceeding his former mentor's achievements in the high mountains

1983

Though Hinault wasn't to know it at the time, 1983 and 1984 would see him needing that same spirit more than at any time in his life. The same knee that had interrupted his steamrollering towards the record books in 1980, and that appeared to have completely recovered such a short time after, finally gave up the ghost that May after his winning ride in the 1983 Tour of Spain, a tough, three-weeks-long race that Hinault had won previously in 1978. Surgery was ultimately decided on, but already a depressed and very frustrated Hinault had decided to give the 1983 Tour de France a miss – a devastating blow to the whole of France, which feared Hinault's progress to that fifth victory would never now be realized. It was with an incredible irony that Hinault's successor was to be found from within his own team, a likelihood so remote at the start of the Tour, that not one French journalist so much as mentioned the name of Laurent Fignon in preview stories of the race.

Not that Hinault showed much interest anyway: all he wanted to do was get the operation out of the way that August, and then prepare for his comeback the next year. Yet Hinault's 1983 had more surprises in store. The self-assurance that Hinault developed after winning the 1980 World Championships had pitched him into a personality clash with his team-manager of eight years, Cyrille Guimard. Now, after Fignon's sensational Tour victory, the final clash was inevitable, with Guimard's former efforts to pacify Hinault happily shelved as he relished nurturing his young protégé's talents. Hinault too, felt little need to stay any longer, and so 1984 saw the remarkable career of 'The Badger' enter its third – and last – chapter in the colours of La Vie Claire, the team he'd put together himself during his six months' convalescence.

1984

It was during the period between 1984 and 1986 that Hinault's proud disposition was most evidently revealed. After a sometimes despondent five-month build-up, during which Hinault needed to reach further into the depths of his courage

As reigning world champion, Greg LeMond made his Tour de France début in 1984, riding in the same team as Fignon who was defending his Tour title against a highly motivated Hinault and possibly LeMond himself. It took just a week for Fignon to establish his right to sole leadership of the French team, and for LeMond to realize his future lay with another team altogether. The young pair pose unconcernedly side by side at the pre-race presentation in Bondy, Paris

and determination, a win in the prologue time-trial of the 1984 Tour seemed to indicate that the great man was on his way back; the young pretender, Laurent Fignon, was 3 seconds slower – first round to Hinault! But then his long lay-off began to have its effect, and soon Hinault was forced to give way to Fignon's all-round strengths in time-trialling and his astonishing ability to burn off the opposition on the long, mountain-top finishes that were a feature of the 1984 Tour. For the first time in his life, and at nearly 30 years of age – when most cyclists are past their prime – Hinault found himself facing defeat, and from another Frenchman! But it didn't stop him having a go in the mountains, notably at L'Alpe d'Huez, a regular host of Tour finishes, which that year staged its most riveting battle: a three-way dust-up between Hinault, Fignon and the eventual stage-winner, Colombia's Luis Herrera. Though Hinault ultimately lost the Tour on that stage, losing a full 3 minutes to Fignon, and being passed by four others including America's Greg LeMond, his bravado in the face of adversity won him an unlikely ally in the French public. For the first time since he'd won the 1978 Tour, the people of France once again took Hinault to their hearts. But this time around it was because he was the underdog.

But Hinault wasn't remotely interested in their adulation – only in redeeming his former status as a four times winner of the Tour de France. Showing himself to be the true champion he was, Hinault swallowed his pride in public, expressing his favour for the way Fignon had taken his second consecutive Tour. But all this time, Hinault was quietly cultivating his adrenalin, letting his legs do the talking for him as the world watched his every move. As if to warn his rivals that Hinault was far from beaten, he showed great tenacity in the final time-trial by taking third place, 3 seconds ahead of LeMond, and so maintained his overall second place by 1:14 over the American. It was 23-year-old LeMond's first Tour, but already his talent was there for all to see. Little did the American know then how much his presence would affect Hinault's final years as a cyclist, indeed affect the whole history of the Tour de France.

Above: Robert Millar, rediscovering the good form he'd used to win a stage in 1983, *en route* to a brilliant win at Guzet–Neige in the 1984 Tour

Left: The strain shows on Hinault's face during the midway point of the 1984 Tour, when Fignon began to take hold of the race. The Breton, at L'Alpe d'Huez, explains to France-Inter radio his reasons for attacking on the toughest stage of the Tour

A completely rejuvenated Hinault set up his last Tour victory in 1985 by storming to a marvellous prologue time-trial win in Brittany. He too had noticed the benefits to be gained from using sophisticated aerodynamic equipment and clothing

1985

In a complete reversal of the 1983 situation, it was Laurent Fignon who was absent at the start of the Tour in Brittany in 1985 as Hinault won a fifth Tour de France prologue. Sadly, like Hinault before him, Fignon had damaged some tendons through, it was said, overuse of cortisone – rumours the Parisian was quick to scoff at. At least Hinault's convincing ride at Plumelec – a pretty village near his Yffiniac birth-place – went some way to compensate a French public that had eagerly awaited a clash of the Titans. Hinault's morale was further strengthened a few days later by his La Vie Claire team's win in the 73-kilometre team time-trial, an outstanding accomplishment for this still young squad that now had

LeMond amongst its members; Bernard Tapie, the businessman behind the new team, had wanted LeMond to join up in 1985 to project his and his company's American business interests. LeMond was eager to take up Tapie's offer and when Hinault gave his willing consent – with a vow to groom the American as his successor – the deal was concluded.

Meanwhile, Hinault's general well-being stood him in good stead for the long time-trial to Strasbourg at the end of the first week. Following a devastating performance at close on 50 kilometres per hour for the 75 kilometres, he seemed to have the race in his grasp. His nearest challenger in the test had been Ireland's Stephen Roche, riding in his third Tour, who still lost nearly 2½ minutes, and overall Hinault led his team-mate LeMond by about the same margin.

Such was the belligerence of Hinault following that outstanding stage win, that, in a similar vein to his 1980 world's victory, the Breton set about taking the 1985 Tour apart – his pride was in danger of running away with him. A few days later he attacked with Luis Herrera on the Pas de Morgins climb that took the race out of its brief sortie into Switzerland. Though still 70 kilometres from the Avoriaz finish,

Eric Vanderaerden's Raleigh team were the nearest challengers to Hinault's squad in the 73-kilometre team time-trial. Following in Vanderaerden's slip-stream is Steven Rooks, riding in his first Tour de France

Hinault, with the help of his pencil-thin companion simply rode away with the Tour, arriving at the modern ski-resort above Morzine with an overall advantage over LeMond of 4 minutes, a gap that he widened further two days later in a 32-kilometre time-trial at Villard-de-Lans. Had he continued at this rate, the 30-year-old Frenchman would probably have exceeded his 1981 Tour-winning margin of 14½ minutes, but the statistics show another story. When Hinault pulled on the final Yellow Jersey in Paris on 21 July, he'd salvaged a meagre advantage over LeMond of just 1 minute 42 seconds. And 'salvage' was a fitting way to describe a final week that, to a battered, bewildered Hinault, must have seemed more like a month.

His unprecedented troubles stemmed from a crash the very next day after his Villard-de-Lans time-trial win. It happened in the last 300 metres of the stage to St Etienne which left Hinault face-down on the blistering tarmac. By his own admission, he wasn't badly hurt – just a broken nose and a gashed scalp. But he was to encounter breathing difficulties for the next three or four days, a factor that almost lost him the Tour to LeMond. Meanwhile, the French public gulped sympathetically when television and newspapers carried pictures of his bruised and bloody face. If in the previous year Hinault had won the hearts of the nation with his spirited resistance to Fignon, it was nothing compared with his latest exploit. Overnight, men who had previously shown a strange indifference to Hinault, rose from their seats whenever television screened the incident once again, while women who had previously considered Hinault to be too cool and aloof, instead found themselves attracted to his roguish new look, with two black eyes and a cluster of stitches across his nose. From that day on, Hinault it seemed could do no wrong in the public's eye.

Though he lost the final time-trial of the race to LeMond, Hinault's prowess against the clock undoubtedly won him the 1985 tour

With his face revealing the extent of his torment and confusion over the whole affair, LeMond arrives in Pau after the final mountain stage with the knowledge that he must wait another year for a chance to win the Tour de France

Hinault's distress was largely attributed to the attack by Spain's Pedro Delgado who took off on the Tourmalet pass – a brilliant stage for victory at Luz-Ardiden

The public's open adulation of Hinault hadn't gone unnoticed by LeMond – that very same day he'd moved ahead of his own challengers, finishing nearly 2 minutes before Hinault had made his dramatic entrance on the Cours Fauriel. LeMond was soon to be faced with a dilemma in the Pyrenees, when he found himself in a position to take over the Yellow Jersey on the stage to Luz-Ardiden, following the near collapse of Hinault in the cold, foggy conditions. Only the strictest of words from the team's coach stopped LeMond from actually going for it, a single act that effectively assured Hinault of his fifth Tour de France, for LeMond was chafing at the bit to take the race lead. As a relative newcomer to professional cycling, and one who was not bound by traditional European ethics, LeMond didn't see the necessity to respect Hinault's race and team leadership, as a result of which, difficult times were ahead for both men.

1986

The record books show that 1986 was the year that Hinault's reign finally ended, defeated by the same young cyclist Hinault himself had plucked from American amateur cycling in the autumn of 1980. Striking pictures of their symbolic meeting are still published today, as European editors struggle to illustrate LeMond's American background. The pictures show LeMond and Hinault dressed as two cowboys in the Nevada desert, rifles raised bandit-style to the sky, with Guimard lurking conspiratorially in the background. It had been quite some coup by the two Frenchmen to tempt LeMond into European professionalism at such a young age – the enthusiastic 'kid' was just nineteen at the time – and the former junior world champion soon proved his class by annihilating the opposition to win the 1982 Tour de L'Avenir – a preparatory stage race of the highest calibre intended to mature young cyclists like LeMond. But what a difference six years can make! In Nevada, there had been two gleaming sets of teeth in evidence as Hinault and LeMond clung to each other like brothers; on the final podium in Paris on 27 July 1986, only LeMond's glistening teeth were to be seen – with Hinault's well and truly gritted behind his pursed lips!

LeMond's anguish of the previous year turned to happiness

Hinault had always said 1986 would be his last year of racing. He'd set that date in 1983 stating that he felt that the age of 32 – which he would reach on 14 November 1986 – was a good time to quit. Then in 1985 he'd promised that he'd help LeMond win his first Tour de France the following year. He also insisted that trying for an outright record of six Tour victories didn't interest him. Depending on one's stance, Hinault could be said to have lived up to all three of those statements, or – especially if your name is Greg LeMond – only his intention to retire. With these basic facts at hand, it is easy to see why Hinault's last Tour de France turned out to be the most explosive one in living memory, and one that was to finally expose the fickle character of 'The Badger'.

Hinault had regularly and openly criticized his young team-mate's apparent disdain for European traditions, particularly when it came to year-round commitment. For example, it is

said that LeMond often slipped away to play a round of golf
during the racing season. The Frenchman found it hard to
comprehend how anyone hoping eventually to win the Tour de
France could spend so much time on his feet instead of
relaxing overworked legs. For his part, LeMond had always
insisted that cycling was only a part of his life – that there was
more to life than living like a 'cycling monk', which is how
most European cyclists exist. Statements like this characterized
LeMond as a money-grabbing individual in Hinault's country,
an unfairly imposed slant not helped by his own sponsors, who
wanted to tell the world that they 'owned' the first 'million-
dollar cyclist'. In real terms, LeMond was no better off than
many of Europe's top cyclists – Hinault included – but this
stigma was to have a bearing on his motivation in the 1986
race, when any semblance of trust that had once existed
between the two La Vie Claire men was finally dissolved.

Additionally, LeMond's determination had been quietly
nurtured since that day in the Pyrenees the previous year. He
still felt he should have been allowed to take the race on in his
own way, even if it meant deposing his own team-mate. And
he'd then spoken out so publicly: 'Next year I'm riding to win
the Tour,' he snapped. 'I won't care if he is in the lead. If he
cracks I'll go. . . .' a frustrated outburst – that Hinault was to
calm a little by telling Greg that he'd help him win the next
year. However, nobody but LeMond himself really believed
Hinault was just going to let the American ride away from him.
From the start of the 1986 Tour, which began on the western
side of the French capital, through to the 21st stage that
ended atop the Puy de Dôme, Hinault engaged LeMond in a
dour duel, one that intimidated most outsiders from even
taking sides, let alone joining in. As far as these two were
concerned, the other 208 cyclists need not even have bothered
turning up!

Both men had arrived at the start in peak condition, with
many experienced observers remarking on Hinault's excellent
well-being. As each day of the race unfolded, so too did each
man shed another robe of defence until, at the mid-way point
of the race before the Alps, they were down to a bare-boned

Using the very latest in aerodynamic componentry, Hinault strengthened his psychological hold over LeMond by winning the Nantes time-trial in the first week of the 1986 Tour by just 44 seconds

fight. Hinault gained early advantages in the Prologue time-trial in Paris, followed by the time-trial at Nantes one week later, where he managed to beat LeMond by just under one minute in 61 kilometres, an advantage gained largely from a front-wheel puncture sustained by the American. At this stage, a still naive LeMond actually believed Hinault's pledge in the pre-race build-up – that he was only riding for LeMond. Hinault, the master of psychology, was in his element here, keeping LeMond guessing as to his real intention, and effectively pegging back any resistance the 25-year-old might otherwise have shown. If LeMond had been able to peer into a crystal ball and read *Memories of the Peloton* (Hinault's autobiography that was published by Springfield Books in 1989), he would have known exactly where he stood. In a passage referring to his last Tour, Hinault admitted: '. . . my style of riding seemed to captivate the public. I was there for the glory and I made no secret of it. Some people didn't like it but I wanted to enjoy my last season and my last Tour. I could afford to spare no effort. . . .'

It took twelve stages for LeMond finally, almost belatedly, to make up his mind about Hinault; on the first mountain stage of the race, Hinault shot away 91 kilometres from the finish in company with another team-mate, Jean-François Bernard and Spain's Pedro Delgado. LeMond didn't know what to do: whether to chase, and risk bringing all his rivals up to the front of the race again, or to trust Hinault's stated tactics – that of drawing out the opposition, an act that would certainly benefit LeMond. Unfortunately, by the time he'd come to a conclusion, Hinault and Delgado had eked out a 5-minute lead, dropping Bernard in the process. By the time Delgado had outsprinted Hinault at the finish in Pau, the stubborn Frenchman had become race leader by a handsome margin. Next day began no better for LeMond, as Hinault, riding like a man possessed – and in a manner in excess of anything he'd ever done before – attacked on the descent of the mighty Tourmalet pass, throwing the Tour de France and the plans of LeMond into turmoil.

Thirty kilometres later, he'd taken a three-minute advantage over the main field, as the Peyresourde climb began to rise up. At that moment LeMond thought he'd lost the Tour: his trusted, self-imposed mentor had an overall lead of eight minutes – and the race was only half over! Fate, however, was to play a large part in Hinault's downfall. For the first time in his cycling life, Hinault's pride-driven impulsiveness backfired on him: he'd forgotten his 31 years, overestimating his strength and stamina, and had underestimated the growing maturity of his American heir-apparent. The weakening French idol was forced to await his pursuers before the top of the Peyresourde, and soon lost all hope on the next, final climb to Superbagnères. There was some justice in LeMond's eventual stage win at Superbagnères, involving as it had done the complicity of LeMond's new American team-mate Andy Hampsten. The previous day, the two Americans had watched Hinault use Jean-François Bernard as a foil to get away. That afternoon, when Hinault began to crumble, Hampsten offered himself as a decoy for LeMond to break away to Superbagnères, an unselfish deed that saw LeMond gain more

A compatriot of Hinault and in his first Tour de France, Jean-François Bernard added to LeMond's uncertainty about his team's likely support when he won a brilliant solo victory into Gap on the eve of the Alpine stages

Switzerland's Urs Zimmerman was a surprising third overall in the 1986 Tour, thanks largely to his ability to follow the wheels of both Hinault and LeMond in their efforts to reign supreme. Since then the farmer's son has not proved to be a serious challenger

than 4½ minutes on the 'treacherous' Hinault, and move to within 40 seconds of the Yellow Jersey, that fabled piece of clothing that, just one hour earlier, had seemed to be slipping away from LeMond for ever.

Being the great competitor that he is, however, Hinault showed himself to be far from down when, three days later, on the eve of the Tour's entry into the crucial Alpine stages, he blatantly joined in a mid-stage attack with third-placed Urs Zimmerman of Switzerland. Though that escape was later nullified by other teams, it seemed to LeMond that Hinault had sided with Zimmerman deliberately to thwart his ambitions. To Hinault of course it was all great fun, and while he undoubtedly slept well that night, his suspicious stablemate was far from happy. But again, Hampsten managed to raise LeMond's pre-stage morale – the depressed Californian had seriously thought of quitting the race during the night – to such an extent that LeMond simply took flight on the Col d'Izoard, one of the most famous passes in Tour fable. With

The Colombian journalist on the right blows a whistle to augment the noise Latin-Americans expect to hear over their radio-sets accompanying the race commentary. His colleagues are no doubt relaying news of the Hinault–LeMond battle

LeMond went Zimmerman and two or three others, while behind, Hinault was driven to despair by his sudden loss of strength. And to inflict further humiliation, his right knee had become sore again, forcing him to grit his teeth with every pedal-stroke. Weeping with his torment, Hinault came close to abandoning the race on the Col d'Izoard that humid afternoon. Only his pride stopped him – trailed as he was by an armada of photographers' motorbikes waiting for such a moment, he couldn't think of stopping. Such was the media interest in Hinault's distress that few of the photographers seemed interested that LeMond was riding away with the 1986 Tour. To them, it was something far more exciting that they were witnessing. Hinault knew this Tour was slipping away from him now; he'd used his strength, his stamina, his experience – and every trick in the book – and all that was left to him now was his dogged inner strength. The spirit that had flared so brightly at the beginning of the decade now seemed little more than a glowing ember.

Incredibly, even though LeMond had come out of the first Alpine showdown with a commanding lead, Hinault continued to interfere in the American's triumphant progress towards Paris, taking control of the most prestigious stage the very next day to L'Alpe d'Huez, by constantly attacking. His strategy was two-pronged: to wrest second place back from Zimmerman and, more importantly to his bruised ego, see to it that LeMond would not achieve the acclaim he so obviously deserved. Hinault simply couldn't bear to see somebody else shine in HIS Yellow Jersey! And sure enough, he stole the limelight all the way to Paris, firstly, by 'escorting' his companion all the way to the top of the Alpe d'Huez mountain, where the two heroes arrived together, their arms held aloft in a united victory salute; but behind their smiling faces, lay a hidden bitterness. Hinault later claimed he could have left LeMond for dead if he'd so wished, a statement that left the LeMond camp incredulous. But Hinault had achieved part of his target – the support of the French public. LeMond might win, but Hinault was making sure he would be perceived as a worthy champion.

One of the most poignant moments in Tour de France history . . . refusing to be overshadowed by his protégé's tremendous ride the day before that took the Yellow Jersey off Hinault's back for the last time in his career, the charismatic Frenchman dominated the showpiece stage of the 1986 Tour to L'Alpe d'Huez by deliberately pacing LeMond in a stirring breakaway. Riding for all the glory he could muster, Hinault knew at this stage that his brilliant career was finally drawing to a close . . .

And that's how LeMond's victory was received by a doubting French public. Their thinking, fuelled by an array of the most partisan journalism imaginable – even in France – was that LeMond would never have won if Hinault hadn't devoted so much energy into helping him. They believed too, what Hinault said in the papers every day: that LeMond wasn't capable of being the team-leader yet, or that he wanted to see how far he could push the young American – 'to see if he had any guts.' These mocking statements were bandied about the La Vie Claire hotel each evening, as, with each passing day, other members of the team slowly, unsurely, took sides in this internal strife. As a result LeMond's nerves had been in shreds for much of the second half of the Tour, his confidence swaying like a pendulum as each new twist in Hinault's psychological game manifested itself. It was impossible to imagine the two battlers actually sitting opposite each other in the dining-room each evening, and it was no great surprise to learn, on the eve of the final time-trial at St Etienne, that the LeMond camp within the team had arranged their own eating plans. Even the management seemed split by the conflict; the Swiss team-manager, Paul Köechli – the same man who'd forbidden LeMond to attack in the Pyrenees the previous summer – had finally thrown in his consent for LeMond to be team leader, while Hinault's former team-mate Maurice Le Guilloux the assistant manager, threw in his lot with the French party.

By the time the two men arrived at the final time-trial stage, the only remaining question was whether Hinault would inflict one final humiliation on LeMond by beating him in the 58-kilometre test. That he duly did – but by only 25 seconds – must have driven LeMond to the depths of despair, for it was plainly obvious that he would have won but for a stupid, nervous fall halfway around the course that necessitated a change of bikes shortly after. Of course, it seemed to the French to be yet another judgement on the ability of LeMond to justify himself as a worthy Tour winner: in France at least, Hinault was still the champion.

And so the reign of Bernard Hinault ended on the Champs

A jubilant LeMond sprints to the summit of the Puy de Dôme with just two days to go to the finish, having at last shrugged off the attentions of Hinault

Hinault wasn't the only one bowing out of Tour de France competition; Holland's Joop Zoetemelk – the reigning champion of the world at the age of 39 – completed his sixteenth and last Tour, finishing in a lowly 24th place nearly one hour behind LeMond. Zoetemelk's weathered face – seen here at Superbagnères – seems to mirror the passing of the years and the memories of seeing Merckx, Hinault and LeMond ride away from him. Hopefully his own 1980 victory is the sweetest memory of all . . .

Literally glowing from the applause bestowed on him by an adoring public, and with more than a hint of a self-satisfied smile on his face, Hinault approaches the summit of the Puy de Dôme in a style befitting his super-star status, and on this, the last mountain he would climb as a professional cyclist. The Frenchman was one of the few men whose charisma outshone the leading climber's jersey!

Elysées at approximately 4.30 p.m. on 27 July 1986, after the most riveting Tour de France in years. Hinault had gone out the way he'd wanted – in glory. The world will never really know if he actually intended going for a record sixth win; to this day Hinault denies this was his target, though the facts of his 1986 defeat would seem to indicate something to the contrary. Maybe it *was* just the fact that Hinault hated to accept he was beatable, for had he not spent his entire career with the sole aim of winning as his motivation? All that can be known for sure about this incredible athlete is his track record in the Tour: 28 stage victories – 72 days in the Yellow Jersey – 5 overall victories. This is a record second only to Eddy Merckx. The brilliant, turbulent career of 'The Badger' was over.

ON A WING AND A PRAYER

The majestic scenery of the Pyrenees provides the perfect backdrop for the competition to find the 'King of the Mountains'. Holland's Steven Rooks ensures the Polka-dot Jersey and his status as best climber in the 1988 Tour are given full credence

At a point 8 kilometres from the summit of the Col du Burdincurutcheta, the road rises at its steepest gradient to a shelf overlooking the Nive valley, and across into Spain. It also affords a clear view down the climb from where, beyond a double-bend in the road, the strung-out peloton rides into view, driven by a cluster of lithely built men riding in an arrow-formation at the front. Prominent because of its position, already well behind this group, is the Yellow Jersey worn by France's Martial Gayant, but even that symbolic piece of clothing is ignored as the leaders step up the pace, stringing out the line of cyclists behind them like a human piece of elastic. Today is the first mountain stage of the 1987 Tour de France, and these men, mostly of Colombian or Spanish origin, have been waiting for this day, and for this mountain for eleven days. No more quivering in the pack for these riders now, no more boring time-trials, no more frightening pile-ups to worry about, no more intermediary 'Catch'-sprints – only mountains, dozens of them, and in varying degrees of difficulty. This arena will be the playground for the men of the mountains for the next 7–10 days.

For the men setting the lung-burning pace on this climb, 'The more difficult, the better it is' would seem to be the motto. Every few hundred metres, one or another rider jumps away from his rivals, teasing them with his enthusiasm at having at last reached his beloved mountain territory, teasing them too at the ease with which he's riding. But he'll soon be brought to heel by the others, soon replaced by another, equally enthusiastic man. The exuberance of these climbers on the Burdincurutcheta was there for all of us to see, and to sigh at the ease with which they can climb higher, faster, than 90 per cent of the men in the Tour. Of all the men in this Tour, none can climb higher or faster than Colombia's Luis Herrera. This tiny 26-year-old, whose physique more resembles that of a sparrow than of a world-class cyclist, is exalted in his own country as if he were an Emperor. In 1984, when Herrera became the first amateur in the history of the Tour to win a stage, hundreds of thousands of Colombians filled the streets of Bogotà in the middle of the night to pay homage to

On a wing and a prayer . . . with his face revealing an unusually high level of effort, 'Lucho' Herrera takes off at the foot of the Alpe d'Huez climb in the 1987 Tour. Is he going for a stage win – or the Tour itself? With a climber such as Herrera, nobody but the gods themselves can provide the answer

'Lucho', their newly crowned *campione*. In defeating the combined might of Laurent Fignon and Bernard Hinault that day at L'Alpe d'Huez, Herrera's win heralded an influx of South Americans into Tour de France legend. The following year he was to return as a professional and win two more stages, and take home with him the title of 'King of the Mountains'. Since that day in 1984, the very title, King of the Mountains, has suited just one man and if others were fortunate enough to win, it was only because 'Lucho' had come to the Tour not fully prepared. The fact that Herrera had been stopped in his tracks from winning a second title by Hinault in 1986, made this first day in the mountains particularly interesting, for this winged angel had come to win.

The race was on by the time the leaders started the long, straight rise away from the bends towards the Burdincurutcheta, and the Yellow Jersey was nowhere to be seen, no doubt sent backwards by the increase in speed from

Spectators fill the slopes above the Col d'Aubisque in the Pyrenees in the hope of catching a glimpse of their climbing heroes

One of the most stirring
sights of the 1987 Tour
– Mexico's climbing sen-
sation Raul Alcala, his
jersey ripped open to
the chest in an effort to
breathe more easily,
makes light work of a
climb in the Pyrenees,
while behind him the
field is in ribbons. It
would take all of Luis
Herrera's stamina to
wrest the jersey away
from Alcala – possibly a
Tour winner in years to
come

Men of the mountains: with Raul Alcala riding free up on the road ahead, Herrera, Hampsten and Millar (*right to left*) raise the pace on the Col Bagargui, their spindly arms and legs taking on a special strength on the sharp ascent. Behind these three can be seen the grimacing faces of Pedro Delgado, Stephen Roche and Switzerland's Beat Breu, for whom the mountains have arrived a little too soon

the climbers. Attention was now centred around five men who were really letting rip on the steepest section of the climb. Suddenly, despite their own brisk pace, a single rider shot ahead of the group, his flamboyant jersey identifying him immediately: Raul Alcala. In less than 100 metres, the Mexican cyclist had opened a significant gap over the other four men, of whom one – Herrera – cautiously gazed ahead to where the figure of Alcala danced away. Alcala had already been wearing the climber's Polka-dot Jersey for more than a week following an aggressive day in the hilly Vosges region, and with this acceleration was making it clear he had every intention of keeping it. Nobody amongst the climbing fraternity had then seemed too concerned at this young man's efforts – 'Don't worry, we'll wait till the Pyrenees,' they said.

Showing them he really meant business, Alcala began to eat up the road in front, pedalling with such a supple motion that one really had to stare closely to see if he was even out of breath! Alcala is not typical of most climbers – his stocky legs and chest tend to remind one of Hinault when he was young – but his fluid style of riding makes it all look so ridiculously easy. And here now in the Pyrenees he was making the other climbers seem pedestrian in comparison; dark-brown legs turning effortlessly beneath a compact trunk, with broad shoulders supporting a supremely proud head. His bright, alert eyes stared ahead in concentration, giving little hint of the effort his body must be making as he strove to pull away from Herrera and the others. By the time Alcala had reached the summit of this nearly 4,000-foot-high (1,135 metres) pass he'd built up a lead of more than one minute – and added another 25 points to his leading total. But Herrera was sure to react.

The Colombian did just that on the very next climb, the Col Bagargui, triggering off a staggered pursuit behind Alcala by up to a dozen others, most of them hopelessly caught up in the fight for the Polka-dot Jersey between the two climbers from Central and South America, yet still willing to combine forces and snub Alcala's brashness, realizing too that his stamina would soon be a spent force – racing in the mountains requires a certain level of caution. Herrera didn't

The winner of the 'King of the Mountains' is traditionally given his equivalent weight of whatever product the competition sponsor manufactures. Here, just before the final stage of the 1987 Tour, Luis Herrera is 'weighed-up' for his value in coffee-beans by race director Xavier Louy. It was appropriate that a Colombian should win the competition sponsored by Café de Colombia, though this ceremony carried more jollity in the years before 1986 when a chocolate company was the sponsor . . .

actually catch his prey for another 80 kilometres, on the final climb of the day, and only after Alcala had gleaned more precious points on the Bagargui and Col du Soudet. Herrera then issued a chilling reprimand to his unexpected rival, by attacking with five others and leaving the Mexican behind on the road to Pau.

Next day was even worse for the spirited Alcala, with Herrera himself setting a torturous pace on the mighty Col d'Aubisque, and almost winning the stage to the ski-resort of Luz-Ardiden. Alcala lost 4 minutes to Herrera on that stage as well as his treasured climber's jersey, a loss that seemed to exemplify the gamble that chasing the Polka-dot Jersey entails. It seemed the 23-year-old youngster from Monterrey had inadvertently chosen the wrong year to take Herrera on, for the coffee farmer's son from Fusagasuga was proving to be in his best-ever form, and in the course of the coming week would pick up high-scoring points on most of the high mountain passes as well as placing in the first five on all of the summit-finish stages. Not surprisingly, with that consistency, Herrera finished in a best-ever fifth overall in Paris, yet his supremacy in winning his second 'King of the Mountains' title was thanks in no small way to young Alcala, who dared to challenge the 'Emperor of Colombia'.

Challenges like that from Alcala are an intrinsic part of the competition to find the best climber in the Tour. The 'Grand Prix de la Montagne' – to give it its French title – is based on points allocated on designated climbs, both on the flatter stages where certain hills carry nothing more than a token value, and most especially in the mountains, where the real points are to be won. Each hill or mountain is rated according to its height, length, severity, and proximity to the finish, with the lowest value being 4th category, and the biggest – 1st category. The most famous and most difficult mountains in the Tour are often given 'hors-catégorie' ('beyond-value') status: climbs such as the 6,935 foot (2,114 metre) Col du Tourmalet and 6,008 foot (1,735 metre) Luz-Ardiden in the Pyrenees – and in the Alps, the mighty Col du Galibier (8,684 foot, 2,647 metres), Col d'Izoard (7,742 foot, 2,360 metres) and L'Alpe d'Huez (6,201 foot, 1,860 metre). Additionally each year, on the highest climb, a rather special award is on offer to the climbers – the 'Souvenir Henri Desgrange', a 10,000-franc prize in memory of the founder of the Tour. It's on mountains like these that the real spirit of the Tour climbers is to be found, and accordingly interest in the competition is at its greatest here – as also is the inspiration of the competitors! Points are allocated to the first fifteen riders over the summit of an 'hors-catégorie' – with 40 points to the first one across – while a 4th category affords just 4 points to the first of just three riders.

There's a kind of romance in the very nature of their quest to become the best climber, an enviable one born out of every man's desire to be able to pedal a bicycle uphill without undue distress. To withstand the stress of scaling 8,000-foot mountains whilst having the air sucked out of your lungs entails certain God-given powers, which very few cyclists are lucky enough to possess. Inevitably, even fewer cyclists can manage to do this with any regularity, which attracts an altogether different envy and curiosity towards men like

It's not all sun, rocks and blue sky. The charm of the aptly named Col de Joux-Verte is there for all to see as the 17th stage of the 1981 Tour de France approaches its final obstacle before Morzine. The Yellow Jersey is worn by Bernard Hinault, the spotted one by Lucien Van Impe

Herrera and Alcala, for whom the mountains in the Tour de France are often their only way of expressing themselves. A considerable amount of this envy comes from within the peloton itself, where all but the élite few quiver at the thought of pedalling through the Alps and Pyrenees for day after torturous day. Because of this high regard, each designated climber is afforded the same protection from his team as if he were potentially a Tour winner – which in some instances he may well be! The perils of racing in a tightly packed bunch are an occupational hazard for all the 200 cyclists in the Tour de France, but for the wee, small climbers, the hazards are exaggerated by their inability to spot dangers on the road ahead, and by their nervousness at feeling hemmed in by other, bigger riders. It's for this reason that many climbers fall, literally, by the wayside before the mountains are even sighted, and the reason why a good team is needed if the climber is to arrive at the foot of the first mountains intact and raring to go.

The degree of competition for the climbers' prize varies from one year to the next, and is influenced as much by the topography of the route as it is by the quality of those taking part. It has happened in the past, that an average, all-round roadman has won this prestigious award, not through his ability at high altitude, but because he's been clever and tenacious enough to win points on the hills that count towards the competition on the flatter stages. Bernard Vallet of France did just that in 1982, defeating notable climbers like Switzerland's Beat Breu and Holland's Peter Winnen – the two men who between them had won the three biggest mountain stages. It was significant that it had happened in 1980, too, when on an unusually weak course all-rounder Raymond Martin came out the winner, ahead of such unlikely names as Ludo Loos and Ludo Peeters – the latter more at home on the flatlands of his native Flanders! It's to be expected that the real climbers are only inspired when the terrain is really tough, and to this extent, the Tour organizers seem to have learnt the errors of their ways, and in recent years given Herrera the challenge his talents deserve, just as his predecessor Lucien Van Impe was given it.

Few men have ever had as much 'presence' in the Tour de France as that which Van Impe attained in the 1970s and 1980s – indeed only the true 'greats' like Merckx and Hinault could be considered in the same context. The Belgian cyclist, who actually comes from the hamlet of Impe, near Aalst in East Flanders dominated the Tour de France climbing scene for all of fourteen years, and during that time won the climbers' competition six times, a record-equalling tally that would have been higher had Van Impe's earlier years not pitched him against the great Eddy Merckx. With a most exquisite riding style, and ever-smiling, intelligent face, Van Impe became regarded as the epitome of what a professional cyclist should be, with an always immaculate racing kit to match his boyish good looks. Probably more than anybody else before or after him, Van Impe's charisma and dedication has brought the King of the Mountains competition increased attention from public and media alike and ensured his successors some deserved acclaim.

The little Belgian's influence reaches across two decades, with climbing victories as widespread as that over Merckx himself in 1972, and lastly over Fignon in 1983 – and that at the age of 36! What is interesting to note, is that the very year he actually won the Tour – 1976 – Van Impe lost what would then have been a fourth climbing title, by just one point! His beneficiary, a virtually unknown Italian called Giancarlo Bellini, must have scarcely believed his good fortune when he heard Cyrille Guimard – the same coach who was soon to take Hinault under his managerial wing – order Van Impe to forfeit his habitual chase for climbing points in order to save his energy for the Yellow Jersey. Sadly, 1985 was Van Impe's last Tour altogether and at 38 years old he was in no fit condition to compete against his climbing heir, Herrera. To have two true climbing 'greats' competing in the same period is a rarity to match that of any Anquetil–Poulidor battle for the Yellow Jersey, and with Van Impe having already stretched his reign beyond fulfilment, we will never know what the outcome of any clash between these two might have been. Still, though neither Herrera nor Alcala has ever raced against Van Impe at

Lucien Van Impe of Belgium has probably done more for the fame of the Tour de France climber than any other cyclist in modern times. Even burly road sprinters envied the grace and style with which Van Impe conducted himself during his fourteen Tours de France. Here, the legendary 'lowlander' sprints up a small hill in a time-trial stage of the 1981 Tour

his best, they will have read about his legend, seen photographs of his glorious riding style, and taken their inspiration from that; for without doubt Van Impe is one of the greatest climbers the Tour de France has ever seen.

The statistics show that only seven men have won the climbing prize *and* the Tour at the same time, a surprisingly small ratio when one considers that the very requirement of a Tour winner is to outclimb all his rivals in the mountains. But when you study that élite list you see the very greatest names in the history of the sport – with three surprising omissions: Louison Bobet, who won the Tour three years in a row between 1953 and 1955; five-times winner, Jacques Anquetil; and none other than Bernard Hinault. Certainly nobody has done it since Merckx managed it twice in 1969 and 1970, a fact that gives a clue to just how difficult it is to ride hard in the mountains all day, every day. Some riders can climb well some of the time, a Tour de France winner has to climb well all of the time, but what sets a 'King of the Mountains' winner apart from the rest is that he must outclimb everybody on every mountain, all of the time, or at least until he's intimidated his rivals into submission. This is no mean feat if you consider that in the 1989 Tour – felt by many to have had the toughest route for years – a total of twenty-one recognized Cols (mountain passes) had to be contested, including one as a time-trial, and five as finishing climbs.

A climber with ambitions of winning the Polka-dot Jersey will have a strategy all worked out before the race even begins. He will have studied especially the itinerary of the mountainous stages, and even taken a week's altitude training before the Tour if he needs to familiarize himself with any unknown territory. When he arrives at the start of the race, he will be able to take a mental note of who his likely rivals are going to be, and, in the days leading up to the first Cols, study the form of those same men to decide his first move. He'll have had to take special care that none of those rivals has tried to steal a march, by chasing points on any of the hills before the mountains are reached. This doesn't usually happen if a legendary climber like Herrera appears to be on form, for his

Bernard Hinault and Luis Herrera provide early roadside spectators with a stirring view of the Tour de France in mountain country on the climb to Avoriaz in the Savoie Alps. Only the race director's red car and privileged television motorbikes are visible as they trail the climbing pair – soon, however, the road will be lined by thousands of screaming spectators

The 1987 Tour found Luis Herrera in best-ever form. Here on the Côte de Laffrey the Colombian sets a pace that only a few can follow – (*left to right*) Delgado, Roche, Lejarreta (obscured), and Bernard

Seen here wearing the Polka-dot Jersey on the Alpine summit of the Col d'Izoard, Robert Millar was a reasonably secure leader in the climbers' competition – until he got caught up in the dog-fight between Greg LeMond and Bernard Hinault in the 1986 Tour. Such was the ferocity of the pace they set on the climbs, that Millar eventually lost his lead in the competition, contracted bronchitis and finally retired from the race . . . a mere shadow of the man who won this competition in 1984

presence is usually enough to stifle all but the least realistic of men – not that the likes of Herrera would degrade their élitism by chasing insignificant hill-primes!

No matter how well a climber has prepared himself mentally, until the first mountains have been climbed he won't know how his body is going to react. In the mountains, more than at any other time, a cyclist's resistance is exposed to the severest test of its capabilities, and so many climbers and potential Tour winners have seen their chances evaporate into the thin atmosphere of the Pyrenees and Alps. Adequate training, conditioning and diet are prerequisites of any cyclist, but if a climber finds himself lacking by the minutest detail in any one of these elements, he won't stand a chance in the hostility of the mountains. Thus it is that the first few climbing days will quickly establish the real candidates for the King of the Mountains competition. Racing in the mountains requires more than just the inborn ability to exist on rarefied air. Experience counts as much as conditioning, and on a stage that might contain five major climbs, timing is essential in the race across the summits – go too quickly, too soon and you're likely to 'blow', just as Alcala did in 1987, with the added penalty of ruining not just that day, but several days after as well. The mountains have a habit of draining a man's resources sometimes more than he realizes.

Right: Displaying a contrast in styles and facial expressions, Dutchmen Steven Rooks and Gert-Jan Theunisse show America's Andy Hampsten how it should be done on the Col du Tourmalet in 1988. Despite their strained faces, the two recent winners of the mountains competition are climbing the famous pass in the Pyrenees by its northern route – the easier side!

Far right: The 1989 Tour was illuminated by a superb individual climbing effort by Holland's Gert-Jan Theunisse. His powerful physique and haunting eyes are noticeable as he speeds towards the summit of the Col de la Croix de Fer in the Dauphine Alps

The successful climbers are those who conserve their efforts on the earlier Cols, risking their energy only to sprint ahead in the last kilometre of each climb before awaiting the others on the descent. Then, as the stage moves into its last third, when the majority of riders are tiring, the top men strike out from further back on the last climbs – the ones that often carry the most points – and try at the same time to inflict maximum damage on the others. This is most typical when the stage actually finishes at the top of a mountain, when few dropped riders can ever fight back! Inevitably, at this stage in the day, a King of the Mountains contender will have his plans influenced by those riders going for overall honours in the Tour. This is where it helps to have something extra left in reserve, for a potential Tour winner will have bided his time thus far, totally ignoring the climbing competition and therefore arriving comparatively fresh towards the end of the stage. The stronger, better prepared, more intelligent climber anticipates the strategy of the overall contenders, and allows himself to infiltrate any late move these men might make. What makes Van Impe, Herrera, and more recently Theunisse so formidable is their ability to win stages of the Tour as well as the climbers' prize, by picking up points during the day, then still have the strength to capitalize on others' efforts.

Theunisse, from Oss in Holland, the 1989 winner of the climbers' prize, demonstrated his phenomenal prowess on the stage to L'Alpe d'Huez. He'd laid claim to the same competition the previous year with a feast of consistent climbing, but then a stupid doping infringement robbed him of any chance he may have had to oust his pal and team-mate Steven Rooks from the Polka-dot Jersey; 1989 was to be

different. The tall, lean rider had already donned the colourful jersey after the second Pyrenean stage to Superbagnères midway through the 23-day race. But it was on the toughest stage of the Tour that Theunisse left a memorable impression on everyone, taking points on the early climbs of the Col du Lautaret and its big sister, the mighty Col du Galibier – the highest point of the Tour – before setting off on the long descent of the Col de Télégraphe with a small group of non-climbers who were looking for a head-start on the main contenders before the last two vicious climbs reared up.

Clearly having earmarked this day for a most special effort, Theunisse had even taken the precaution of putting a team-mate in this group to help maintain the pace down the long, windswept valley that led to the foot of the gruelling, but undeniably pretty, Col de la Croix de Fer. No sooner had this climb entered a narrow canyon, reached through a short unlit tunnel, than Theunisse simply rode away from his flabbergasted companions, pounding his long legs like pistons, despite the fact that the finish was still 68 kilometres away! Up amongst some of the most enchanting scenery the Tour had seen that year, Theunisse's vivid red-and-white-spotted jersey provided a fine image as it flew past the thousands of densely packed spectators towards the 6,784 foot (2,068 metre) summit, to begin an equally inspiring descent through wooded forests and past crystal clear mountain lakes. On this breakaway of epic proportions, Theunisse displayed not just superb climbing skills, but also the ability to ride alone for a great length of time – and still keep enough in reserve for obstacles like the 14-kilometre monster climb that is L'Alpe d'Huez. He'd also chosen his moment well, knowing that behind him, a battle royal was imminent amongst the three protagonists for overall victory – Pedro Delgado, Greg LeMond and Laurent Fignon – and that he could take advantage of their unwillingness to chase.

Theunisse's long, flowing locks streamed out in the turbulence his slim body was creating. At 45 kilometres per hour, he powered to an 8-minute lead across the Verney reservoir that fills the bowels of the Romanche valley. It was at

At 8,684 feet the Col du Galibier has in recent years been the highest pass in regular use by the Tour

Although he's yet to show his true class, Andy Hampsten is potentially the most talented climbing specialist around today and would surely have won the climbers' prize already if he didn't nurture ambitions to one day win the Tour. Here he is seen against a suitably enticing Alpine background, as he approaches the summit of the Col du Galibier in 1989, no doubt thinking of the finish at L'Alpe d'Huez – still 135 kilometres and two 'hors-catégorie' mountains away . . .

Stephen Roche and Pedro Delgado benefited enormously from having Luis Herrera in this group on the road to Villard-de-Lans in 1987, having just left race-leader Jean-François Bernard behind. Charly Mottet shares the pacesetting with Herrera while Roche, Delgado and Marino Lejarreta bide their time

the end of this innocuous-looking valley that the final climb began, with its steep road containing 21 hairpin bends, forcing Theunisse to dig deeper still for the reserves that could carry him to a magnificent stage victory. Cheered on by the hundreds of thousands of screaming Dutch people who take their annual holidays there especially for the Tour, many of whom ran alongside their hero with fresh water and encouragement, the elegant rider achieved his greatest ambition to date – a win at L'Alpe d'Huez and final securement of his Polka-dot Jersey! Unfortunately, such was the excitement about the outcome of the race behind him, that Theunisse's efforts that scorching-hot day will never be truly recognized – unless this 27-year-old with the strikingly good looks can one day win the Tour de France. The Dutchman's efficient style of riding seems certain to make him a contender for overall victory in a year or two, and at the very least change the popular waif-like image of a King of the Mountains winner. By anybody's standards, his victory that day was achieved with the most outstanding physical effort – possibly even more outstanding than that made by a certain American rider in Paris four days later.

Whether or not Theunisse does expand on his climbing talents, and one day win the Tour, his possession of the climbers' prize – following on from Rooks, who became the first Dutchman ever to win the award – lends support to the growing belief that we may never again see a thoroughbred climber like Van Impe or Herrera become King of the Mountains. The Tour is simply becoming too competitive to allow the little climbers to ride away in the mountains, which is partly the reason why Herrera has only won two King of the Mountain awards in his six attempts to date, and why he's only secured a miserly three stage victories. Some people feel that Herrera has not fulfilled his true potential. Certainly the Colombian attracts a lot more adulation and respect than would normally be afforded to a 'mere' two-times winner of this competition. But when his climbing ability became so obvious with that historic stage win in 1984, from then on nobody dared give him much freedom, fearful of the damage he might cause! Other factors hinder Herrera too, none more so than the fact he rarely races in Europe, and therefore gains little in the way of experience at riding against powerful team-work. Herrera spends an average of two months a year in Europe, usually riding the Tour of Spain as a warm-up to the French race – he won the Vuelta in 1987 – or taking in the Tour of Italy instead.

1987 was definitely Herrera's best Tour, though nobody would have been more disappointed than himself that he didn't win a single stage (he came second on two occasions), while his ride to L'Alpe d'Huez with less than a week to go must merit as highly as that which won him the same stage in 1984 – as well as proving that the Colombian could have been a Tour winner. It was also the day young Alcala made one last effort to regain lost pride. Alcala had raced ahead of Herrera and the main Tour contenders on the flat Romanche valley in company with Fignon and Anselmo Fuerte of Spain. The trio arrived at the foot of the gruelling L'Alpe d'Huez just over 2 minutes ahead of Herrera, Delgado, Roche, and Spain's Marino Lejarreta, but more than 5 minutes behind Fuerte's team-mate Frederico Echave, who'd broken clear much earlier to prepare the ground for his young team-leader. The race became a thrilling pursuit match between some great riders with greatly differing ambitions; four men – Echave, Fuerte, Fignon and Herrera – going for the stage win; two men racing for the Tour itself – Roche and Delgado; and one man rallying for one last time for the climber's Polka-dot Jersey – Alcala.

Although Echave clung on to win by a reduced, but comfortable, margin from Fuerte, it was Herrera who lit the match behind as he sprinted away at the very foot of the climb. When he went, nobody dared follow, and initially it seemed the Colombian was going not just for the stage, but for overall victory as well! Only Delgado kept Herrera in check, with a gap that grew to 15 seconds a third of the way up, then dropped to 10 seconds at the halfway point. Behind these two, Roche, Lejarreta and America's Andy Hampsten were nearly a minute down despite the Irishman's desperate efforts to hold Delgado, who by now was preparing to pass Herrera with 6 kilometres to go – just as the Colombian was steaming past a conceding Alcala, and now had Fignon in his sights too! Then Delgado began to struggle, with the effect that Herrera raced gleefully past again and dropped the Spaniard completely 2 kilometres before the finish, with Fignon going backwards now, and just the final few bends left to negotiate. Herrera wheeled into the broad, panoramic finish-straight still more than 3 minutes behind stage winner Echave, but the

The rugged looks of Fabio Parra (here at Luz-Ardiden in 1985) are in sharp contrast to that of his more angelic-looking countryman, Luis Herrera. But perhaps the university-educated Parra is a more likely winner of the Tour overall

In 1987 Parra chased his compatriot Herrera to Luz-Ardiden as both of them sought this prestigious stage victory. Jean Claude Bagot of France illustrates the agony of trying to keep pace with a climbing specialist!

damage he'd caused will never be forgotten by those who tried to follow the Colombian's pace. It even seemed to have finished off Roche's overall ambitions on that one mountain – for his pace-setting aided only Delgado, who'd been strong enough to withstand the pressure. It's a sad fact that if Herrera had been a better tactician, and if he'd had a European-style team to control the racing for him, that ride to L'Alpe d'Huez could have ended with him – and not Delgado – wearing the Yellow Jersey.

When Herrera eventually retires, which is something he's always threatening to do, the Tour de France will miss this elusive character, perhaps more than some people realize. Though he's never attained the presence that Van Impe had, the effort his frail and very vulnerable body makes trying to emulate the Belgian climber, will leave a poignant memory for millions of cycling enthusiasts around the world. At least Herrera has rekindled the tradition installed by the legendary climbers before him – that to ascend to a King of the Mountains throne, one must secure at least one stage win in the mountains as well, just as it is expected a Tour winner should also prove his all-round prowess by winning a mountain road race stage. Hopefully, Theunisse's example in 1989 signifies the continuation of this belief, as it has added so much more respectability to the climbing competition in modern times. And it would be a fitting acknowledgement of Herrera's initiative, if his countryman and fierce rival Fabio Parra were to take up the challenge on behalf of South American cycling. With two stage wins to his credit so far, and a third overall in the 1988 Tour, Parra might perhaps one day win the Tour, something that Herrera dreamed of many years ago.

Thanks to the superhuman exploits of riders like Van Impe and Herrera – and especially the highly talented men who dared to challenge the two 'Kings' – there's a special place in everyone's heart for the men of the mountains, and for the prize they so agonizingly seek. For them, and for those who one day hope to emulate them, awaits the call: 'King of the Mountains!' – there could not be a more fitting and well deserved title.

HEROES

On a warm, balmy afternoon in the summer of 1985, the noise of 500 journalists pounding typewriters could be heard coming from the *Salle de Presse* in Pontarlier's sports recreation centre. Less than one hour earlier those journalists, now frantically engaged in compiling their race stories, had watched the Danish cyclist Jørgen Pedersen win the day's stage, the tenth of that year's Tour de France, and just 90 seconds later had put pen to paper to record the fact that Bernard Hinault and Greg LeMond crossed the finish-line together in company with the majority of the year's Tour favourites.

It was these men – Hinault, LeMond, Luis Herrera of Colombia, Phil Anderson of Australia, Spain's Pedro Delgado and Ireland's Sean Kelly, as well as Pedersen – that the journalists were now writing about, prior to despatching the stories to their editors around the world. Those stories would tell in detail the way in which Pedersen had emerged triumphant after leaving behind seven others in a break that had developed in mid-afternoon. Attention too would probably be drawn to the continuing dominance of this Tour by Hinault, and how his teasing attack immediately after the day's start had helped intimidate his likely rivals.

Few, if any, of those stories will have mentioned the plight of the English cyclist Paul Sherwen, who was riding for the La Redoute team. That morning, as the field rode away from the historic town of Epinal, Sherwen spotted a team-mate of his losing his balance as the bunch slowed to take a tight bend. Ever the perfect colleague, Sherwen managed to stop his mate's imminent fall by holding onto his jersey – only to find himself falling onto a metal crash barrier at the roadside. With heavy bruising to his lower back and shoulders, as well as a banged head, it was a few minutes before Sherwen summoned the wherewithal to remount his cycle and rejoin the race.

On any other day of the Tour, Sherwen would have achieved a swift return to the sanctuary of the peloton – but not this day; almost in the same moment that Sherwen was being tended by race doctor Gérard Porte as he lay at the side of the road, Hinault accelerated away from the front of the

Paul Sherwen's agony didn't end at Pontarlier: his 'reward' for surviving was to haul his exhausted body over five mountains the following day in order to keep his place in the Tour. He's seen here using every last ounce of energy to ride up the last climb to Avoriaz, where he finished just inside the time limit. He owed his reinstatement at Pontarlier to one man – Albert Bouvet – the most sympathetic of the Tour's officials and himself a former Tour rider. This was enough to ensure Sherwen's utmost commitment, not least because the highly respected Bouvet had implored Sherwen not to embarrass him by abandoning the race in the next few days! Sherwen eventually finished the Tour in 141st place – nearly 3½ hours behind the winner, but with his pride intact

race, apparently amusing himself in the first few kilometres of this 204-kilometre stage. Four or five minutes later, as Sherwen began to pedal again, Hinault was still pulling clear, panicking his rivals' teams into a frenzied chase. So it was that the Cheshire cyclist – riding in his seventh Tour de France – found himself alone, several kilometres behind the race, as, ahead of

Holland's Ad Wijnands rode through most of the 1985 Tour with a mass of bruises covering his face following a fall in the first week of the race. But his troubles were to be largely ignored by a media more interested in the deeds of the leading riders

him, Hinault propelled his breakaway group and the strung-out bunch at more than 60 kilometres an hour as the road dipped and rose in the Jura region of the country.

Soon it became obvious that Sherwen was suffering badly from the effects of his fall, and two of his team-mates – Regis Simon and Alain Bondue – dropped off the back of the speeding bunch to help their stricken companion. Even though Hinault finally desisted from his attack after 15 kilometres, the peloton maintained its high speed, causing further problems for the La Redoute trio. On learning of their continuing deficit, Sherwen unselfishly ordered his friends to leave him, lest they should all be eliminated by the end of the day; the race rules include a clause that any rider finishing more than a certain percentage slower than the stage winner (depending on the speed and terrain of the stage) risks immediate expulsion from the race.

Despite their insistence, Sherwen refused to allow Bondue and Simon to waste themselves – by now, nearly 20 kilometres into the stage, the peloton were still riding nearly two miles an hour faster than anything Sherwen could muster – and reluctantly the two Frenchmen set off to limit their own losses, knowing already that they stood little chance of catching even the tail enders of the race by Pontarlier. For Sherwen it was to be the loneliest and most painful ride of his life: 'I knew I would be eliminated at the end of the day,' he said later. 'But I didn't want to end my last Tour in this way.' So on Sherwen cycled, with just the escort of a single Gendarme's motorbike ahead of him on this road to nowhere, and the *camion-balai* (broom wagon) hovering behind him, its driver anticipating the inevitable – that Sherwen would abandon before the day's end, yet encouraging him at every opportunity. 'Having that truck behind me all day actually helped,' Sherwen recalled afterwards. 'That would be a very undignified ending . . . like going out of the world's greatest bike race by the backdoor.'

Three-and-a-half hours later, at the point where Pedersen started the winning break of the day with 66 kilometres to go, Sherwen was more than one hour behind the race and still suffering badly with his bruised back, a situation that made it difficult for him to sit down on his saddle for any length of

A stage winner can be a hero too! Norway's Dag-Otto Lauritzen, a hefty all-rounder more suited to the flat stages, flabbergasted Tour followers, and team-mates, and himself by holding out to win the feared Pyrenean stage to Luz-Ardiden in 1987, arriving just seven seconds before the star climber of the race, Luis Herrera. Knowing his inability to climb fast, the former commando in the Norwegian Royal Marines set out more than 100 kilometres earlier to build himself a substantial lead before the gruelling final climb which he survived despite some ferocious attacking by Herrera, Fabio Parra and Andy Hampsten. His stage victory was undoubtedly the most audacious of the whole Tour – and his winning gesture reflects the glorious hysteria a feat such as this can provoke

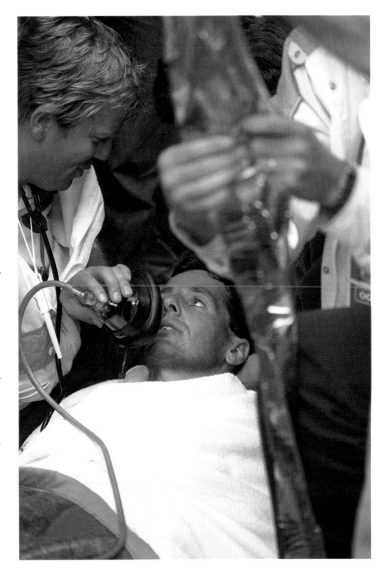

There are heroes, and then there are heroes. . . . One of the most publicized incidents of heroism came in the 1987 Tour, when Irishman Stephen Roche collapsed at the end of a tough Alpine stage to La Plagne and went into oxygen-debt. It was his frail body's reaction to an exhausting day at the end of an exhausting week that had seen Roche and Pedro Delgado constantly battling for victory in the Tour. Roche's courage took on a whole new meaning a few days after his collapse, when he trounced Delgado in a time-trial to win the Tour as one of its most worthy victors

Having won the summit prize on the Col des Saisies, and at a pace which infuriated the peloton's 'hierarchy', Martin Ramirez promptly crashed on the very first hair pin bend of the descent – much to the raucous delight of those who had scorned his 'anti-social' behaviour on the last mountain stage of the 1987 Tour. Despite his injuries, Ramirez rejoined the race and went on to finish in Paris – in 13th place!

Henrik De Vos somersaulted over a precipice on a mountain descent in the 1987 Tour – emergency services were mustered to retrieve him from where he landed, and the Gendarmerie helicopter airlifted him to hospital. Despite his long fall, De Vos wasn't seriously injured and was racing again a week later in Belgium

time. When Pedersen crossed the finish line on the Larmont hill high above Pontarlier at around 4.20 p.m., Sherwen was still 40 kilometres away, doggedly persisting despite the odds stacked against him. By the time the Tour de France's 500-strong armada of journalists had returned to their seats in the *Salle de Presse*, Sherwen had still not reached Pontarlier – let alone the long, winding climb to the 1,210-metre-high finish. Only later, as the telex machines started clattering their first emissions to newspaper offices, did the plucky Englishman start to climb the finishing hill.

By the time he reached the summit 7 kilometres later, only a single timekeeper and his La Redoute *directeur sportif* were waiting. If any journalists had been able to wait this long, they couldn't have failed to be moved by the sight of Sherwen weeping in the arms of his manager, Raphael Geminiani, as the full emotion of his courageous task broke through the mask of fatigue on his face. On what later turned out to be the second fastest *en-ligne* stage of the race – and on a hilly stage at that – Sherwen had ridden almost by himself for all but 4 kilometres of the 204-kilometre leg. He'd finished well over an hour behind the stage winner, and 26 minutes outside the official time limit. In total, Sherwen had resisted his own suffering for nearly 6½ hours, principally to avert the professional cyclist's most humiliating fate – a ride to the finish in the *camion-balai*. Yet so admiring were the race officials of Sherwen, that they waived their right to exclude him from the mountainous stage to Morzine-Avoriaz next day. The 28-year-old had survived the toughest day of his life – and made a true Tour hero of himself in the process.

The Tour de France image to the outside world has always been one of heroes, and heroics. Some, like Sherwen, receive little or no media attention, while others become international celebrities. In 1983 Pascal Simón rode for six days with a cracked shoulder-blade while wearing the Yellow Jersey, before eventually retiring in the Alps. And two years later, Hinault's spectacularly filmed crash on the streets of St Etienne – where the Breton broke his nose and needed fifteen stitches for a gushing head wound – created a place for him in the French nation's folklore. But there are heroes, and then there are heroes. Both Simon and Hinault, courageous as they were, were able to share their suffering with a passionate French public, knowing that the publicity received was of immense image-building value in the coming years. For the most part, it's the lesser known men like Sherwen who evoke the most respect. For them to suffer, usually means for them to suffer alone.

Transparently, it would seem that becoming a hero in the Tour de France isn't really all that difficult, for with the physical demands involved in just taking part, each and every one of the cyclists is a hero of sorts. Each of the 200-odd athletes sets out with the intention of finishing in Paris — indeed all of them will have had to plan their whole season around it. Yet, as each successive stage of the Tour can be treated as a single race in itself, the season-hardened constitution of the professional cyclist is always threatened; wind, rain, sun, hills,

This hero is not forgotten. Jacques Goddet lays flowers at the memorial to Britain's Tom Simpson on the exposed slopes of Mont Ventoux — just above the exact spot where the courageous cyclist collapsed and died during the 1967 Tour. Though Simpson's death was largely attributed to drugs he'd administered to hide pain, his story is no less romantic, and serves as one of the most poignant in Tour de France history

Seen here cresting the summit of the mighty Col du Glandon in the 1988 Tour, this group of non-climbers, led by Britain's Malcolm Elliott and Italy's Bruno Leali, know what it's like to survive in the Tour. The haunted look on their faces says it all . . .

Tough times lie ahead for this Colombian cyclist after a fall in the first week of the 1988 Tour. Though a race doctor is spraying a 'second skin' onto his delicate wounds, it will be many days before he can sit comfortably on his bike

After racing day in, day out for a fortnight, crashing twice in the process, then hauling his massive bulk through three tough Pyrenean stages, it's no wonder Eric Heiden's face reflects the true torture of trying to finish one's first Tour de France. The Olympic speed-skating champion who won seven gold medals at the 1980 Lake Placid winter games, has just arrived at the summit of Superbagnères, nearly 6,000 feet above sea-level, knowing he still has to survive two horrendous Alpine stages before he can afford to breathe a sigh of relief. A few days later he crashed on the descent of the highest mountain in the 1986 Tour – the Col du Galibier – and was helicoptered to hospital

cobbles, crashes, mountains – all these elements are what a professional cyclist encounters in his daily work-routine throughout the season. What makes the Tour so draining – and such a challenge – are the additional problems that racing the Tour in mid-summer entails: the heat, so suffocating in the mountains, while debilitating on the long, flat stages; and the regularity with which large sections of the peloton are felled by some horrendous crashes.

But it's the mountains that represent the biggest challenge to a Tour cyclist. Sometimes for days on end, the race will cross and recross the Alps and the Pyrenees, creating new heroes – those that can climb freely – while destroying the morale and physique of others, whose energy has been spent in just reaching the mountains. It's this last mentioned group, whose expressions can be readily studied as they haul themselves up to 8,000 feet, and down again, with the pain etched into their sweat-caked faces, that epitomises the Tour de France hero.

Blending all this together in a melting-pot of drama, anguish and – for some – success, there is the intensity of competition, the pressure of sponsors' expectations, and the personal ambitions of the top stars. It's the competition that

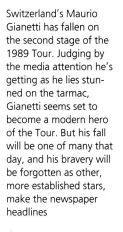

Switzerland's Maurio Gianetti has fallen on the second stage of the 1989 Tour. Judging by the media attention he's getting as he lies stunned on the tarmac, Gianetti seems set to become a modern hero of the Tour. But his fall will be one of many that day, and his bravery will be forgotten as other, more established stars, make the newspaper headlines

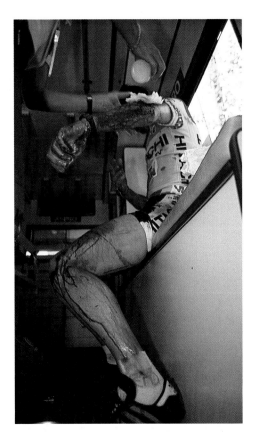

Jos Haex lost so much skin after a crash in 1989 that although he managed to finish the stage to Montpellier, he was forced to quit the Tour because of his injuries

A heavy crash on the cobbles of the 3rd stage to Wasquehal in 1989 left Britain's Sean Yates with deep cuts to his arms and legs. Yet so hard was the 29-year-old's adrenalin pumping, that he carried out a solo pursuit of the speeding bunch for nearly fifteen kilometres. The scars from that crash are still in evidence

exposes the very essence of a Tour de France cyclist, whether a potential Tour winner, or a rider with the never-say-die attitude of a survivor. To understand what it is that inspires men like these to perform as they do, it's necessary to dig deep into the history books, where tales of tragedy and personal suffering are plentiful, and where glorious sepia photographs remind us of where the roots of the Tour de France cyclists really lie. For present-day heroes of the Tour have much in common with men like Maurice Garin, the winner in 1903 of the first Tour de France, and Eugène Christophe, who donned the first Yellow Jersey ever awarded, in 1919, and whose misfortunes have subsequently become a timeless fable. But more than anything else, today's Tour hero breathes the same spirit as those men Garin and Christophe beat, men who rode merely to say they finished the Tour de France, the toughest sporting event in the world.

'Convicts of the Road' is a most apt description of the Tour de France cyclists. It is an expression first used in the Tour's earliest years but one which holds as much weight today. A touching *esprit de corps* is evidenced as two Belgian cyclists share a bottle of water on the long, hot road to Gap in the 1989 race

RACE FOR THE GREEN JERSEY

From 300 metres away it had seemed as if a sandstorm was blowing up. Only at 250 metres did it become clear that this billowing cloud of dust contained a seething mass of humanity. And now, still 200 metres from where we stood, the glistening alloy of wheels and handlebars became distinctly clear – almost 200 cyclists were bearing down on us at great speed. The swaying mass flicked from one side of the road to the other, then back again: bicycles and men seemingly banked at ridiculously crazy angles to the ground. Finally, at 100 metres, individual jerseys, but not faces, could be picked out; a white one – probably Guido Bontempi's; the blue-and-white one that could only be Vanderaerden's; the green-and-grey of Van Poppel's Superconfex team; the green-and-yellow belonging to Mathieu Hermans' Caja Rural team; the blue-and-yellow jersey being worn by KAS's Sean Kelly.

Then it was all over in a few short seconds. The figure of Van Poppel became distinct from amongst the swirl of bikes, the Dutchman's familiar bulk already a clear length ahead of his 'opponents' – soon the match would be over. All that remained was for Van Poppel to throw his muscular arms in the air as victor, in the same stance as that of a winning prize-fighter. What had set out as an apparent mirage, had in fact been for real; another bunch-sprint finish to a stage of the Tour de France had just ended.

What these men were fighting for – literally – in Besançon in 1988, was the right to wear the Green Jersey that denotes the leader of the points competition within the race. Based on accumulated points that are awarded to the first twenty-five finishers of each stage, the Green Jersey is arguably the second most important award in the Tour. Arguably, because the red-and-white Polka-dot Jersey awarded to the best climber in the race is undeniably hard to win. But where the Green Jersey gains increased respect is that whereas a few, carefully timed attacks in the high mountains of the Alps and Pyrenees will often be sufficient to secure a King of the Mountains victory for a specialist climber, anyone hoping to take the Green Jersey outright must compete day in, day out over the entire duration of the race in order to consolidate his position. For the points

competition is on offer to all in the race – not just to the mercurial sprinters.

Until recently, it was quite common for a Tour de France winner to compete for the Green *and* Yellow Jerseys, with points available in the mountain stages and in time-trials too. During his period of reign in the 1970s, Eddy Merckx of Belgium also took home with him the Green Jersey on three occasions – much to the chagrin of the hard-done-by sprinters. The last Tour winner to do the same was Bernard Hinault in 1979, and he too upset the sprinters. Since 1953, when the competition was first created, the Green Jersey has traditionally been the domain of the archetypal sprinters: the men with heavily-muscled arms and legs, and barrel chests, whose fear of the high-altitude mountains, mixed with physical inadequacies for climbing, ensures their vigorous participation in the bunch-sprint finishes. For they can never hope to win the Yellow Jersey outright.

There can be few things more exciting in cycle racing than seeing a Tour de France stage end in a tumultuous sprint. With its sophisticated technology, television shows it all. Those of us watching see it all too, though such is the speed at which a sprinting bunch of cyclists moves that it's impossible for the human eye to read what's happening, or to appreciate the finesse that a road sprinter employs to gain an advantage. To be actually in there is another thing altogether; and it's rare indeed to hear a sprinter adequately or accurately portray what it's really like – largely because, to the Kellys and Van Poppels of the world, it's second nature to be in there.

The way in which the same select few find themselves fighting out the last few hundred metres of a stage with an uncanny sense of consistency, derives from a carefully calculated method. This method, or craft, is handed down from the experience of other sprinters in years gone by and reads simply enough, but in practice it is far from simple: it involves a build-up of speed by the sprinters' team-mates with one hour of the race to go – a collective action orchestrated by the rival sprinters to ensure nobody escapes from the peloton to win. (This same increase in speed can start earlier if a

breakaway group of riders is jeopardizing the favoured plan.) In the last 20 kilometres of the stage the pace increases to leg-shattering speeds – often in excess of 60 kilometres an hour – as the closeness of the finish tempts non-sprinters to chance their luck, only to have the sprinters' teams pick up the pace yet again. During all this time, the ten or so acknowledged sprinters will be riding in the respective shelter of four or five of their pace-making colleagues no more than 10 metres from the front of the bunch.

As the last 10-kilometre stretch approaches, the attacks will start to come – most of them from riders acting as 'decoys' to draw the strength from rival teams' sprinters. As soon as one escapee is caught another will go, usually meeting a similarly swift response from the peloton. If the attacks are allowed to continue, it's inevitable that the sprinters will gradually be left to their own devices – their trusted team-mates simply shelled out of the pace by constant chasing down of the breakaways. However, a wise sprinter will already have ensured that his most faithful lieutenant is kept fresh until the

In Kelly's absence, Belgium's Eric Vanderaerden was udoubtedly the best sprinter of the 1986 Tour. Here the precocious Limburger gets the better of Guido Bontempi (*left*) and Mathieu Hermans at Villers-sur-Mer to earn more points towards his Green Jersey

very final surge. This is where, in the final few kilometres, potential stage winners often lose their place at the front, exposed too soon to the turbulent air created by a pack of cyclists riding at high speed. It's also where the guile and cunning of a sprinter comes into play.

Now, finally, they find themselves pitched against one another, the long-awaited showdown approaching. It's a very lucky sprinter who still has help at this late stage. But there's always one – a support rider who's managed to survive this far – and it will almost certainly be this rider who acts as a lead-out for the sprint itself in the last kilometre, his protected sprinter in line astern, their every move watched by a desperate bunch of men eager to extract some selfish advantage from the situation. With the 'pilot-fish' riding flat-out at the front for his team-mate, the other men in contention take up their favoured positions, selecting their own preferred lead-out man from amongst their rivals. Now well inside the final kilometre, the pushing and shoving begins as the top men seek out the best wheel to follow, happy to oust physically anyone who's in the way – even at 70 kilometres an hour! It's a measure of a sprinter's reputation if he finds himself tracked by more than one opponent. At the same time, the sprinter must take note of which way the wind is blowing; a rider exploding his sprint on the leeward side of the race has considerable advantage.

This is where a crash is most likely, as a hefty shove from a colossus such as Bontempi or Van Poppel would be enough to send an inexperienced sprinter into the fencing – though at this late stage in the proceedings, it's very rare to find any 'intruder' still brave enough to mix it with the top men. It's only in the final 300–400 metres that the jockeying for position stops and is exchanged for the simple tactic of speed, with each sprinter unleashing everything he's got as, for the first time, he senses the finish-line ahead. It's here that a whole day's work by a sprinter's team can end in success if their man has what it takes to come out ahead – if he's got the 'bottle', and with it, the speed. But for everybody else it means defeat, for to come second is of little consolation at this level. Instead, those that lost out today must sleep on their mistakes, nurture

The strain shows clearly on Sean Kelly's face as he seeks the best position for the imminent sprint at Bordeaux in 1985. At the moment this picture was taken with just eight kilometres to go, the riders were travelling in excess of 40 miles per hour and Kelly knows he'll be lucky to move up through the field before the sprint begins in earnest. His steely eyes are no doubt fixed on his main rival, Eric Vanderaerden, who is ten places ahead of him, paced by an erstwhile team-mate. The result – 1st Vanderaerden, 2nd Kelly

their bruised pride – and come out fighting tomorrow. It's certain to make for a great race!

But the battle to be the points winner in the Tour isn't just determined by an ability to sprint – that would be too easy. Not only does our lovable rogue have to pitch his bravery and strength into the frightening mêlée that represents road sprinting, he also must consider how best to survive the high-altitude mountain passes that the Tour de France twice encounters in its annual progress. It's the mountains that are the very essence of the Tour de France, the background to some of the great challenges open to man. But for the heavily built sprinter clad proudly in his Green Jersey, they represent another, less secure environment. For in the mountains there's nowhere to hide, no helping vacuum to be sucked along in. Here, the once bullying sprinter is reduced to a mere mortal.

Many potential winners of the Green Jersey have been known to give up once the flatlands have been left behind, scared of the mountains and scared to expose their inadequacies to a watching world; Eric Vanderaerden, at 21 years, one of the youngest European professionals, quit the Tour in 1983 on the eve of its entry into the Pyrenees, claiming he was happy with the publicity he had gained in his native Belgium for having worn the jersey for most of the first week, but refuting criticism that he was intimidated by his rival Sean Kelly, who that same day had taken control of both Green *and* Yellow Jerseys. Just as a sprinter's psychology can win a stage for him, so must that same will power be employed to coerce him through the torments of climbing 8,000-foot-high mountains. And a good start to one's Tour is all-important, as Vanderaerden's 1986 effort illustrated. With Kelly absent from the race that year owing to a damaged collarbone, Vanderaerden had an increased dose of confidence in him to beat his fear of the high mountains, and arrived in the Pyrenees safely ensconced in his green tunic, with only Guido Bontempi to bother him – should he survive the climbs.

What Vanderaerden did then, and – until 1989 – most sprinters have done, was to get aboard what is affectionately known as 'the bus' – a group formed by the non-climbers to

Eric Vanderaerden had to conquer more than just his rivals' ambitions in 1986: his renowned fear of the mountains was overcome too, and he's seen here warily searching the horizon for the finish of the Alpe d'Huez stage

On the eerie mountain of the Col d'Izoard in 1986, 'the bus' makes its steady progress through the thousands of spectators who have eagerly waited for more than 40 minutes to catch a glimpse of these 'tourists'. The rider in the Green Jersey on the far right is of course Eric Vanderaerden who's safely aboard

Eddy Planckaert – Belgium's 'other sprinter' – failed to finish the 1986 Tour despite giving Eric Vanderaerden a run for his money in Nantes where he beat his rival and team-mate with ease. But the crafty man from Nevele in East Flanders returned two years later to win the Green Jersey, and achieve a lifetime's ambition in the process

counter the anguish and agony of riding alone in the Alps and the Pyrenees. By calculating their progress to precise speeds, 'the bus' carries aboard all who would otherwise be left way behind, their will to survive destroyed. This unlikely union relies for its survival on two factors: its numerical and collective strength – sprinting rivalries are forgotten here – and an ability on the part of one or two of its passengers to gauge, to within a few minutes, its arrival at the finish within the permitted cut-off time. In the tougher mountain stages, this group of men will quickly form at a predetermined location, once its ringleaders have established how the pattern of that day's racing is likely to go. They will know exactly how far from the finish they are, and how fast the leaders might be pedalling; they will then gauge their own pace accordingly – all the time making sure none of their passengers is left behind. It's generally accepted that in any given Tour, there are only two or three cyclists who have the experience and intelligence necessary to 'drive' the bus – to get it there on time! And it's

been known to go wrong in the past; many are the times when journalists, late from leaving the finish area atop a mountain, have been treated to the somewhat amusing sight of fifteen to twenty burly men sprinting for all they're worth in order to beat the clock!

Unluckily for would-be passengers of this very special bus, a shortening of stage-distances in the 1989 Tour meant increased speeds in the mountains by the race favourites. That factor, coupled with tighter controls by officials, who in the past had looked the other way when dropped riders hung onto service-car doors, saw names like Eddy Planckaert, Bontempi, Van Poppel – and Vanderaerden – eliminated from the race in one fell swoop at Superbagnères in the Pyrenees. This was the first time so many sprinters had been taken out of the race since a group of thirty men was eliminated at L'Alpe d'Huez in 1977, and has ensured that in the future there'll be no such

Belgium's Eddy Planckaert won the Green Jersey in 1988 after years of trying. He's seen here with team-mate Alphons De Wolf at his side as 'the bus' in which they have been travelling starts to fragment within sight of the stage finish atop the infamous Puy de Dôme in the Massif Central

thing as an easy ride for Tour de France sprinters. Not that their mountain truce lasts for long anyway: even as they ride side by side in mutual sympathy, so is their more ruthless streak directed towards a few days' time, when, free from this thin-air agony, they'll be seen banging shoulders with each other in the race for the Green Jersey.

Kelly and Vanderaerden have played the starring roles on more than a few occasions in the past. One of their most publicized incidents was at Rheims in 1985. There, on the long avenue that leads to the massive west front of Rheims Cathedral, Vanderaerden – already wearing the Green Jersey – had Kelly for company as the two led the sprint with 200 metres to go. All the way down the straight road, the two men could be seen swerving from kerb to kerb and even throwing punches at each other, while, behind, the other sprinters battled desperately to stay in contact. Both Vanderaerden, who won, and Kelly, were disqualified for dangerous riding; yet such was their speed, even with one hand on the bars, that they finished more than a length ahead of the proclaimed winner, Francis Castaing!

Even if Vanderaerden and Kelly weren't actually sprinting for the stage victory, their rivalry and aggression were undiminished. Here the troublesome two fight for fourth place at Bordeaux in 1984, with Francis Castaing of France completely outclassed

Sean Kelly

Kelly has had more than his share of controversy over the years – more often than not with Vanderaerden – chasing as he has every available point with the utmost conviction, and not a little aggression. His post-race manner with questioners, to whom these days he provides endless answers, no matter how trivial or probing they might be – and always with a pleasant demeanour – doesn't fool anyone: in the past decade, the Tour de France has not had a Green Jersey contender more deadly than Sean Kelly. And without doubt, he's now the wisest cyclist in the whole peloton. When one analyses the points competition in the Tour, it's necessary to consider two aspects: the Green Jersey as won by Belgium's Freddy Maertens for instance, predominantly a sprinter, and the Green Jersey as won by Sean Kelly. The comparisons could not be more different, yet between them, both Maertens and Kelly have dominated the points competition in the Tour de France over the past fifteen years.

Maertens was already the most feared sprinter in the world when he won his first Green Jersey in 1976 – the year before Kelly first raced as a professional, for Maertens' Flandria team. In that year's race, Maertens demonstrated astonishing powers as a short-distance time-triallist – something his protégé, Kelly, would do in future years, only with increased effect. But Maertens was primarily a sprinter and always failed the moment the Tour arrived at the smallest mountain. In Kelly, here was a man who could sprint and time-trial against the best in the world, and whose climbing ability was equal to many of the established mountain men.

While still riding as a super-domestique for Maertens, Kelly won his first Tour de France stage in 1978 at Poitiers, though only against half-a-dozen men – not several hundred. But his second stage victory two years later in St Etienne against just one man – Marino Lejarreta of Spain – held far more significance, for it was achieved after a 35-kilometre escape in the foothills of the Auvergne, and won Kelly increased respect as a feared competitor in all types of terrain. He donned his first Green Jersey after the Nancy stage of the 1982 Tour de

Sean Kelly rose out of Freddy Maertens' shadow to become the most feared competitor for the points competition in the 1980s. Like Maertens, Kelly has won a string of the world's top one-day classics, and the Tour of Spain. He's also been the season's best all-rounder many times. Only the world championship has eluded this legendary character . . . Kelly is seen here in the final few kilometres of the 1989 Tour, just a few minutes from winning his Green Jersey for a record fourth time

Belgium's Freddy Maertens was the greatest road-sprinter of his era, easily winning the Green Jersey in each of the three Tours he rode – 1976, 1978, 1981 – and taking a total of fifteen stage wins in the process. Additionally, the Flemish cyclist won several of the world's top one-day classics, became the World Champion twice – in 1976 and 1981 – and even won the 1977 Tour of Spain overall, with a record tally of thirteen stage wins! But as prodigious as his talents were, drug-abuse and sadly, alcoholism, savaged his health to the point where his country's cycling federation tried to refuse him a licence to race, decreeing that he was an embarrassment to the sport. Maertens story is one of rags to riches to rags, as all that's left of his once considerable wealth is a dingy seaside flat on the North-sea coast of Belgium

1988: having been dropped on the Col de Madelaine, Sean Kelly and Malcolm Elliott face an arduous ride to the finish at L'Alpe d'Huez, still 80 kilometres and two 'hors-catégorie' climbs away! Such was Kelly's collapse that he would shortly become a rather élite passenger on 'the bus'

France – the same stage that won Phil Anderson the Yellow Jersey. When Kelly rode into Paris that year, with the Green Jersey securely fitted, he'd emulated Maertens' final points title of 1981, and laid the foundations for a Tour de France career far beyond the scope of any normal sprinter, thanks to an astonishing day in the Pyrenean mountains that saw Kelly stay with all the Tour favourites – Hinault, Zoetemelk, Anderson, as well as fourteen others – and then outsprint all of them at the finish in Pau. To this day, that stage-win is still probably Kelly's finest.

Ironically, had Kelly not become the complete all-round cyclist he is now, he would surely have won the points competition more often than his outstanding record shows. In winning those early Tour stages, Kelly displayed to the world his growing talents as the complete cyclist. Suddenly Kelly found himself not just a Green Jersey winner, but a contender for overall honours too. But this realization had two drawbacks as far as his sprinting ambitions were concerned.

As far back as that victory in Pau in 1982, Kelly began to believe he might one day win the Tour de France, a belief that hindered his concentration in the bunch-sprints; in a frightening mass sprint, there is no such thing as tomorrow for a cyclist hell-bent on winning the stage. For someone like Kelly

seeking overall honours, 'tomorrow' figured very much in his plans. At the same time, his Green Jersey rivals became alarmed that 'the sprinter's tunic' might be put out of their reach altogether if Kelly was allowed to secure too many points in the daily sprints, a realization that ensured Kelly would find himself severely restricted when it came to landing the 'big' one – a stage victory from a bunch-sprint. In fact Kelly's list of victories in the Tour is woefully short: just five stage wins, and only one of those against a full complement of recognized sprinters – at Fontenay-sous-Bois in 1980.

But it's his incredible tally of twenty second-place stage finishes in eleven Tours de France that says most about the Irishman's achievements. For in all his long years as a professional, Kelly has never benefited from having a team, or team-mate, able to lead him into the sprint itself. Had he done so, who knows how many of those second places would have been firsts? Only in 1989, with PDM, did Kelly get sufficient support at last; and he showed just what it meant to him by taking his fourth points title, a full four years after he'd last won it. Kelly's 1989 performance is without doubt his best ever, despite the fact that he failed to win a stage, or didn't match his fourth place overall in 1985 – when he finished second on no less than five occasions!

The foundations of his ninth place overall in 1989, when he finished 18 minutes 25 seconds down on winner LeMond, is the most consistent stage-by-stage performance by anyone in a modern Tour de France and that includes the likes of Merckx and Hinault. It reads like this, from the Luxembourg prologue through to the final time-trial in Paris: 3rd, 5th, 4th, 8th, 10th, 31st, 11th, 11th, 8th, 4th, 18th, 5th, 15th, 6th, 5th, 6th, 28th, 6th, 5th, 7th, 3rd, 47th. Contained within those placings are rides like his best-ever prologue time-trial; his best-ever ride to a mountain-top finish – at Cauterets on stage 9; and his best-ever mountain time-trial ride – to Orcières-Merlette on stage 15, where he was just nine seconds slower than LeMond.

Only in the three longer mountain stages, the 73-kilometre time-trial to Rennes on stage 5, and the 24.5-

Another Belgian sprinter in the Tour during the mid-1980s was Rudy Matthijs – here disposing of Sean Kelly and Eric Vanderaerden (in the Yellow Jersey) at Vitre in 1985. The statuesque first-year professional seemed destined for a career as stunning as that of his predecessor, Freddy Maertens, when he won three stages in his first Tour. However, Matthijs never raced in the Tour again due to an almost crippling back injury. He's now a taxi driver

The significance of Kelly's retirement from the 1987 Tour is very evident from this picture which shows television cameras hovering like vultures as the Irish legend pedals his last stage to Bordeaux

kilometre test into Paris, did Kelly fail to finish in the top twenty – altogether a remarkable achievement for a 33-year-old. Whether 1989 proves to be Kelly's swansong remains to be seen, but some of his rides then must have evoked memories for him of his earlier Tours, such as 1983, when he finished seventh in the gruelling mountain time-trial to Puy de Dôme, and the next year, when he failed twice to beat Laurent Fignon, that year's Tour winner, in the crucial stages against the clock. In the last of those 1984 time-trials, he came within 0·048 seconds of eclipsing Fignon at the 51-kilometre Villefranche test. Only a scrupulous check of the electronic timing by the French officials stopped Kelly from being declared the winner that day.

Eleven Tours de France must contain a wealth of memories for Kelly, some of them good, but quite likely many bad ones too. For instance, there was the time he lost the Green Jersey in 1984, on the actual finish-line of the Champs Elysées, and the occasion in 1987 when a seemingly innocuous fall resulted in a damaged shoulder and a sorry exit from the race. Some of his memories have been shared by the millions of Irish folk who have followed his every move on television and in newspapers, and by the hundreds of inquisitive, yet admiring journalists whose careers have been blessed with the presence of such a sportsman as Kelly. Yet in the kingdom he's built around himself in the peloton, there'll probably be memories that only Kelly will know of. Maybe one day he'll choose to share these with the rest of the world. Then perhaps we'll really know the story of Sean Kelly and his Green Jerseys.

THE 'NEW WORLD'
MAKES ITS ENTRY

Jean-François Bernard 'easily' won the monstrous time-trial up the slopes of Mont Ventoux. However, his waxen frailty – portrayed graphically in this photograph taken three kilometres from the finish – would soon be exploited to the full by his more experienced rivals . . .

Greg LeMond's staggering defeat of Hinault in 1986, which brought to an end one of the most dominated periods of Tour de France competition, has itself become the catalyst from which a new breed of racing cyclist has emerged – one that has its roots embedded in the 'new world' of cycling, and in countries that are experiencing the rebirth of cycling popularity. Through a near-fatal shooting accident, LeMond missed the opportunity to build on that historic milestone in the sport. Fortunately, a clutch of equally great competitors sprang up to take their place in the fresher, more sophisticated era that LeMond's 1986 victory had begun – little expecting that LeMond would ever return as a serious contender.

1987: Roche continues the trend

The 74th Tour de France started in West Germany for the second time in seven years – with the same financial considerations that attracted the Tour to Frankfurt in 1980 sharing the headlines this time in Berlin, where the isolated city was celebrating its 750th birthday. The fact that the Tour left Berlin from outside the Reichstag, the former Nazi parliament building adjacent to the now-breached wall, and that on the previous day Poland's Lech Piasecki had become the first East European to wear the Yellow Jersey helped to overshadow the

Poland's Lech Piasecki, on the streets of West Berlin, became the first East European to win the Yellow Jersey

Pretty Alsace villages guided the 1987 Tour back towards its mother country

3 million Deutschmarks ($1 million) the city's people had to fork out to put this French show on the road. East Germany's refusal to allow the Tour to pedal its way across their country to its next stopover in Karlsruhe only added to the demonstrative atmosphere, but spoilt what might have been a prelude to the events in 1989, when East Germans finally got their first experience of Westerners' ways.

An action-packed first week saw opportunist stage wins in plenty, and Jean-Paul Van Poppel streaking away with the green points jersey by scoring one win and two second places. The massively long 87-kilometre time-trial on stage 10 set the

Tour up for the Pyrenees three days away, with Stephen Roche beating Charly Mottet by 40 seconds, and France's great hope, Jean-François Bernard, by 1 minute 24 seconds. Pedro Delgado lost 2 minutes 29 seconds, Laurent Fignon 4 minutes 15 seconds, Sean Kelly 5 minutes 1 second, Andy Hampsten 6 minutes 20 seconds and Luis Herrera 9 minutes 1 second! Kelly crashed out two days later, leaving the Tour without one of its greatest characters. America's Davis Phinney was one who didn't mind – he won his second-ever Tour stage at Bordeaux that afternoon, with Britain's Malcolm Elliott in third place. The sprinters gave way to the climbers on stage 13, when Dutchman Eric Breukink helped tow Herrera and two other Colombians – and Bernard – on the dropping road into Pau after the five had ridden clear of Roche, Delgado and Robert Millar in the first mountains of the Tour.

Herrera emerged as a possible Tour contender the next day by finishing strongly on the steep climb to Luz-Ardiden, but Norway's Dag-Otto Lauritzen held the Colombian off by just seven scant seconds for the stage win. Roche lost a few seconds to Delgado, but gained considerable time on Bernard and Mottet, the Yellow Jersey wearer. Hampsten moved up to tenth overall by coming third on the stage. After a torrential storm had flooded the roads of the stage out of the Pyrenees to Blagnac, and Van Poppel had scored his second stage win at Avignon, the time-trial up Mont Ventoux transfixed everyone's minds; all of them were aware that the cruel mountain of the Vaucluse had killed Britain's Tom Simpson exactly twenty years earlier. There were no such tragedies in the true sense this time; but there were personal setbacks for riders like Raul Alcala who lost 9 minutes 41 seconds, Fignon 9 minutes 9 seconds, Hampsten 6 minutes 12 seconds, Millar 5 minutes 14 seconds – all of these men beaten by Bernard who streaked up the suffocatingly hot mountainside with an uncharacteristic aggression to beat Herrera by 1 minute 39 seconds and Delgado by 1 minute 51 seconds, and took over the Yellow Jersey from his compatriot Mottet. Roche moved into second place overall, 2 minutes 34 seconds behind Bernard, despite finishing a 'poor' fifth.

A stunned Jean-François Bernard knows he's losing the Yellow Jersey as he rides towards Villard-de-Lans

A weary Stephen Roche struggles to hold on to his Yellow Jersey on the slopes of L'Alpe d'Huez, having been left behind by Herrera's pace

Next day, stage 19, was the day the Tour de France erupted, with Bernard losing his jersey to Roche after an incredibly active day had seen the French race leader suffer two mechanical problems within a few kilometres, only for Roche and half a dozen others to take full advantage. Fignon and Mottet's Système-U team had provided the manpower, while Roche had instigated this untypical ganging-up on Bernard. The Irishman ultimately escaped with Delgado in the last 20 kilometres to bring the Tour down to a two-man race. The Yellow Jersey changed hands again for the third day in succession after the Alpe d'Huez stage had seen a battle equal to the 1984 one between Herrera, Fignon and Hinault. More than a dozen climbers were involved this time, with one – Herrera – putting the cat among the pigeons by attacking on the very first hairpin bend of this climb. Only Delgado could get anywhere near him, and he survived Herrera's brutal pace – just – because he knew Roche was losing time all the way. The Spaniard was now raceleader by 25 seconds – raceleader for the first time in his career.

This brutal attack by Pedro Delgado seemed destined to win him the 1987 Tour at La Plagne, but the Spaniard over-estimated his strength and had lost most of his hard-earned advantage at the finish where Roche arrived in a state of near-exhaustion

Nobody could have thought this absolutely thrilling Tour could become even better, yet the next day's stage to La Plagne helped to achieve just that. Fignon showed a spark of his former self by easily outsprinting the previous day's second-place man, Anselmo Fuerte, at the modern ski-station. But, as at L'Alpe d'Huez, the stage-winner's efforts were overshadowed by the battle behind. Again it was Delgado and Roche who went to war with themselves and with the mountain, with the Spaniard jumping away in the manner which Herrera had employed the day before. Alas, Delgado overestimated his stamina, and blew up in the last 3 kilometres, to be passed by a storming Fabio Parra, and almost caught by Roche himself in the last 50 metres. Such was the Irishman's exertion, and that after a day that had seen him attacking continuously, that he succumbed to oxygen deficiency at the finish and had to be revived by worried race doctors. Surely now, with Roche spreadeagled on the ground beneath a survival blanket, Delgado had won the Tour?

In 1987 Malcolm Elliott was the star rider of the first British trade team ever to ride the Tour de France. Though the team – ANC – disbanded soon afterwards, Elliott went on to a continental career with a Spanish team, Teka, and became a feared road-sprinter in his own right

Only one more mountainous day to come – the 186-kilometre stage to Morzine, taking in five hard climbs, including the *hors-catégorie* Col de Joux-Plane 15 kilometres from the finish. Not surprisingly, the two chief contenders showed little aggression all day, but with just 39 seconds separating them, both men were looking for a late opening without tiring themselves out before the final time-trial two days later in Dijon. It was Roche who saw a chance. On the sinuous descent of the Joux-Plane, he noticed Delgado hesitating on a tight bend, and put his head down all the way to the finish in Morzine. Delgado, no doubt remembering his fall on the same descent in 1984, when he broke his collarbone, was too cautious this time, and he rolled into the finish having lost 18 seconds of his small lead to Roche. The scales had turned in the Irishman's favour at last.

The confident Roche, an accomplished time-trialist on any terrain, and one who had won the closing time-trial of his victorious Tour of Italy just six weeks earlier, easily beat Delgado for the Yellow Jersey, putting 59 seconds into the sad

Stephen Roche's wife, Lydia, had the biggest smile of all in Paris after her husband had been crowned as the winner. She became much in demand as a highly paid fashion model later that year

but honourable Spaniard in the shortish stage, on roads made slippery by light rain. Bernard salvaged something from his disappointing Tour by thrashing around the 38-kilometre circuit at almost 50 kilometres per hour to beat Roche by 1 minute 44 seconds on the stage. The Irish Prime Minister, Charles Haughey, flew into Paris especially to greet Roche at the finish, and stood hugging him on the podium as the Dubliner beamed all over his cherubic face to an astounded world. Just one month later, Roche's incredible season was capped by a momentous victory in the one-day, 185-mile-long (297 kms) World Championship in Villach, Austria, to make him only the second rider in history – Eddy Merckx of course being the other – to achieve the unique triple of winning Tour of Italy, Tour de France and World Championship in the same year.

1988: Delgado's tarnished gold

Before the 1988 Tour had even begun, the world knew that for the second year running the race would be starting without its previous winner. Roche, like LeMond before him, had been injured since his brave victory the summer before. A troublesome right knee had become damaged again in the winter, and Roche was faced with an uphill struggle no less awesome than that of LeMond's – the American was again absent from this year's Tour, his body still struggling to regain its former strength. A slightly shortened Tour was on the menu in 1988, after the *Union Cycliste Internationale*. (UCI) – cycling's governing body – had declared that the Tour was too long in what was becoming an increasingly congested season for the professionals. But while the purists threw their arms up in horror that such an instruction could be enforced on the world's most important cycle race, the only effect it really had was to make the racing harder and faster; the 91-kilometre first leg, won by Canada's Steve Bauer, proved just that. Despite being held up by striking shipworkers on the west coast of Brittany, and by rain-soaked roads, the hyperactive peloton still averaged 48 kilometres an hour! Though Bauer lost the Yellow Jersey that same afternoon in the team time-trial – to Holland's Teun Van Vliet – the Canadian was to become something of a hero in this Tour by regaining the race lead eight days later, and then, amazingly, defending it almost right through the Alps.

Britain's Sean Yates made a bashful hero of himself too, when he won the 52-kilometre, wind-assisted time-trial to Wasquehal on the Belgian border and put himself within grasp of the race lead. But then the mountains loomed up on stage 11, and ended his ambitions. That first day in the mountains saw Sean Kelly crash for the second year in a row, though this time with less damage, and saw a demoralized Fignon slip back through the field with an unlikely ailment: a one-metre-long tapeworm had grown in his intestines! Fignon retired from the race that night, just a few hours after Colombia's Fabio Parra had scored a marvellous solo victory at Morzine. Kelly and Jean-François Bernard were the other two most

Even before the first real mountains had begun, Sean Kelly found himself in trouble. The out-of-form Irishman lost more than three minutes on this 11th stage to Morzine

notable losers, arriving at the finish nearly three minutes after Parra, and with neither man looking in the best of health.

The Alps came into play next day with the almost obligatory L'Alpe d'Huez finish placed 227 kilometres along an exceedingly mountainous itinerary: two 2nd-category Cols and three *hors-catégorie*! Kelly had already lost more than 10 minutes by the time the race had reached the summit of its first major obstacle of the 1988 Tour – the Col de Madelaine, 6,500 foot (1,984 metres) high. At the front the two Colombians, Parra and Herrera, were keeping the pace high to protect their mountain territory, while Delgado's team-mates lent their support to make sure nobody launched any damaging attacks. It was not until the summit of the excruciatingly steep Col du Glandon with its stretches of 1-in-6 (16 percent) grades that the race leader Bauer began losing ground, and only then because Delgado himself was stirring things up ahead. He attacked 2 kilometres from the summit of this beautiful pass and was joined in an instant by Holland's Steven Rooks. The Tour had come well and truly alive!

The Canadian cyclist Steve Bauer began to nurture serious ambitions of winning the Tour de France during his eight-day reign as race leader. He is pictured here, on the climb to the Col du Glandon, where he was finally dropped, although a brilliant chase brought him back into contention for the final haul up to L'Alpe d'Huez

Fabio Parra in a rare solo pursuit to his stage win in Morzine. The swarthy Colombian became the first South American to make it onto the final awards podium in Paris with his excellent third place overall

THE escape of the 1988 Tour: Steven Rooks leads Pedro Delgado on L'Alpe d'Huez shortly before they were joined by Fabio Parra and Rooks' team-mate Gert-Jan Theunisse. Though Rooks had been away for some 60 kilometres with Delgado, he still had enough fire power to counterattack and win this prestigious stage, while Delgado took over the race lead

Bauer bravely rejoined along the Romanche valley, but not with Delgado and Rooks, for they were nearly 2 minutes ahead as Bauer led the 13-strong group onto the familiar final climb. 'The Alpe' didn't host such a thrilling race as it had done in 1987, but instead saw a stage-end skirmish amongst the press motorbikes, whose antics seemed to be blocking Parra's attacks – the Colombian had caught the two leaders with less than 3 kilometres to go in company with Rooks's team-mate Gert-Jan Theunisse. No sooner had Parra been snubbed for a second time, than the ever alert Rooks profited from the confusion to escape in the slipstream of the motorbikes, bringing the press corps into disrepute with the race organizer later that evening, but bringing himself his greatest ever victory – and the Polka-dot Jersey as best climber. Theunisse was happy too: he crossed the line in second place with his hands high in the air. While the PDM 'twins' celebrated, Delgado donned the Yellow Jersey at L'Alpe d'Huez for the second year in succession – only this time it was for good! A gallant Bauer had discovered previously unknown climbing talents that day, but despite finishing just two places and 1 minute 28 seconds behind Herrera, the Canadian was 25 seconds too slow to stay in yellow for another day. The vicious pace set by the leaders on this 12th stage had finished the hopes of a number of pre-race favourites: Charly Mottet at 8 minutes 3 seconds, Eric Breukink at 16 minutes 55 seconds, Bernard at 16 minutes 55 seconds and Kelly at 23 minutes 46 seconds!

When you look at Bernard's performance at L'Alpe d'Huez, it's even harder to imagine how he managed to almost win the next day's stiff uphill 38-kilometre time-trial to Villard-de-Lans. If Delgado hadn't won a brilliant, authoritative victory there, the Tour might have had an earlier and more sinister scandal than the one that was about to hit the race. For the supposed urine infection that Bernard was claiming had caused him to lose so much time the previous day, couldn't have possibly cleared up in time for the Frenchman to all but demolish the Tour's leading contenders. As it was, Bernard was to pull out on the next stage to Guzet-Neige, as did other well-respected riders like Mottet and Switzerland's Urs Zimmerman

Jean-François Bernard had an inconsistent Tour in 1988. He nearly won a strategic time-trial stage but abandoned two days later, having lost considerable time in the mountains. He's seen here in a significant breakaway to Lievin in the first week of the race

– after the entire Tour entourage had spent Bastille Day flying or driving across the southern half of the country to arrive at the foothills of the Pyrenees. Clearly something was amiss for so many top men to withdraw.

At Guzet-Neige, Delgado's riding continued to display the true allure of a Yellow Jersey wearer when he took another 40 seconds out of Rooks at the tiny ski-resort, and after Britain's Robert Millar had completely fouled up an imminent stage win by following a breakaway companion down a diversionary road for Tour vehicles, less than 500 metres from the finish! Next day, the 187-kilometre stage to Luz-Ardiden took the Tour over the Cols of Mente, Peyresourde, Aspin and Tourmalet, but such was Delgado's stranglehold on the race, that the real action didn't start until the final kilometres of the penultimate climb, where the Henri Desgrange souvenir was the prize for the first rider past the summit – the Tourmalet was the highest point of the 1988 Tour. Delgado's countryman Laudelino Cubino had been given the chance to chase a stage win, and perhaps act as a springboard for Delgado – despite the fact that Cubino was in another team – and Delgado contented himself with sprinting clear of the others to cross the Tourmalet's summit, in the style befitting a Tour winner. But though he was happy to await his companions on the tricky descent, his acceleration had been only a prelude to his effort on the final climb.

In front of hundreds of thousands of frenzied Spaniards who had driven, cycled, walked, even climbed over the hillside from neighbouring Spain, the Segovian roared away with just 3 kilometres to go of this 14th stage, driving himself through a seething mass of humanity. Delgado took third place behind Cubino at Luz-Ardiden and was now more than 4 minutes clear of Rooks with the Puy de Dôme and a final 46-kilometre time-trial to come; it was thought that Delgado might even double his lead before Paris.

Van Poppel reminded everybody that there were other cyclists in the race besides Delgado. The Dutchman took his third stage win at Bordeaux the next day, but any chances he'd nurtured of basking in the limelight that evening soon vanished into the clear Atlantic sky. A television presenter on a post-race programme 'Journal du Tour', had apparently gleaned some information that Delgado had been tested 'positive' at a drugs test after winning the 13th stage to Villard-de-Lans – someone hinted it may even have been the race director Xavier Louy who'd naively let this rumour slip. The cocksure presenter smugly told a stunned television audience that evening of his 'exclusive' news, not caring that the report had yet to be confirmed, and unconcerned about the damage it might do to the race and to Delgado's reputation. To the Spaniards in the race, and to the whole of Spain, it sounded like a nasty smear tactic by the French, who had so little to shout about. Others – including riders such as Bauer and Hampsten – felt Delgado should be expelled if the rumour was found to have any substance.

The proud Spaniard denied he'd taken anything illegal, and next day arrived at the start for the stage to Limoges as if nothing were wrong. But the race itself was in complete limbo, with the riders clearly upset by the attention suddenly thrown on them when the race was all but over. In addition the anxious journalists did not know what to inform their public, such was the confusion from within the organization. It took until the next afternoon for the organizers finally to decide

Just a few hours before a decision would be made on his status within the race, Pedro Delgado issued his own particular response to critics when he burned everybody off his wheel and rode like a man possessed to the summit of the 4,600-foot-high Puy de Dôme. With three kilometres to go, only Theunisse could keep pace with the furious Spaniard – but soon even his legs would melt under Delgado's final acceleration

The Spanish national flag was paraded by an ecstatic Pedro Delgado as he and his team made their lap of honour around the Champs Elysées circuit

what action should be taken, now that the results of Delgado's second urine analysis were available. Half the world seemed to be waiting on tenterhooks for the verdict. That afternoon, as if to show his contempt for those people trying so hard to discredit him, Delgado had taken it on himself to scatter his rivals to the four winds when he launched himself furiously up the steep ascent of the Puy de Dôme and arrived atop the extinct volcano to a massive cheer from the thousands of Spaniards who had postponed their return home especially to support Delgado in his hour of need. A deep sense of relief was felt later when it was announced that the substance he was alleged to have taken was Probenicid — a drug that can act as a masking agent for anabolic steroids, or, as Delgado insisted, a drug he had used to flush uric acid from his system. Others pointed out that Probenicid is also a cure for gout — not a common ailment among athletes. Either way, as the drug wasn't yet on the proscribed list of banned substances — it was to become so a few months later — no action could be taken against the race leader, as quite simply under the rules at that time he'd done nothing wrong.

And so the Tour was allowed to continue on its way again, too late to rectify the damage inflicted on its image, and too late to eradicate the slur on Delgado's name; but continue it did, with most people happy to see such a proud, dignified cyclist as Delgado become the winner of the 75th Tour de France. He did his best to win the last time-trial around the Burgundy wine region, failing by just 11 seconds, but increased his lead over second-placed Rooks to more than 7 minutes, a gap that proved his was a masterful all-round performance to match any that Hinault had achieved in his long reign. Perhaps the most significant thing about the whole affair was that the next October, at the presentation for the 1989 Tour, it was announced to a packed audience that a former journalist, Jean-Marie Leblanc, was to be the new race director – Xavier Louy had been sacked! Though no reason was given, it was generally felt that the Société du Tour de France – the company that owns the race – had held Louy personally responsible for the whole sorry affair. The flamboyant Louy is now running as a politician in his beloved Dordogne in the west of France.

1989: LeMond returns from the dead

Still tingling from its image-bashing of a year earlier, and accordingly with an increased media presence, the Tour set up camp in the tiny city of Luxembourg, with Delgado again the race favourite following his narrow win in his own national Tour of Spain earlier that spring. But incredibly, as if his troubles the previous year hadn't been enough, the 29-year-old Spaniard caused the hundreds of journalists to stare disbelievingly at the result sheets of the 7·8-kilometre Prologue time-trial. The reason was that Delgado had finished last – 2 minutes 54 seconds slower than Eric Breukink the stage winner! Stupidly, Delgado had mistimed his warm-up for the opening defence of his title, arriving at the starting-ramp 2 minutes and 40 seconds later than his designated time. Rules being rules, the clock kept ticking until the shocked rider emerged from a scrum of television cameras and reporters to take his place in the race. The fact that competitively he lost only 14 seconds to Breukink is testimony to the form Delgado had nurtured for his defence.

It was inexplicable that such an experienced cyclist could allow this to happen, and no less inexplicable was his next 'suicide-act'. The following day, through insufficient eating, Delgado found himself unable to keep pace with his Reynolds team-mates in their team time-trial over 46 kilometres. The bewildered Spanish riders finished last of the 22 teams, after waiting frustratedly for their stricken leader, who was now nearly 10 minutes down on general classification after just two days' racing! It was at this stage that the more humorous scribes began teasing about what a great script the organizers had drawn up for this year's race. But nobody could then have foreseen just what an incredible Tour they were about to enjoy, and how Delgado was to play such a strategic role in it all. It all started three days down the road from Luxembourg, after a lively though inconsequential trek through the Belgian Ardennes, across the cobbles of French Flanders, before the airlift across northern France to Dinard in Normandy, where the eagerly anticipated 73-kilometre-long time-trial would take place.

Until within a few minutes of the last rider finishing – Portugal's Acacio Da Silva, who'd worn the Yellow Jersey since winning the opening road stage in Luxembourg – Delgado looked to have hit back in the most forceful way possible, by winning this revealing leg of the race. But then America's Greg LeMond arrived, dressed like a Martian with his aerodynamic helmet – sensation! The almost forgotten star had beaten the revitalized Spaniard by just 24 seconds to take over the Yellow Jersey for the first time since his victory in Paris three years earlier. Now, journalists didn't know what to do about this latest sensation: whether to shower praise upon Delgado, who had proved he was far from being down and out – or to hail LeMond's startling victory as a complete resurrection, following almost three years of pain and anguish. Their unusual dilemma wasn't helped with Fignon coming in third, within a minute of the flying American. Perhaps he too should be singled out for attention? Other things were more definitive: Herrera lost 9 minutes 6 seconds, his compatriot, Parra, 4 minutes 38 seconds. For these two men, as for Stephen Roche and

His face a mask of desperation with the knowledge that he's already lost more than two minutes for arriving late, Pedro Delgado hurtles around the eight-kilometre time-trial course for the Luxembourg Prologue

Charly Mottet who'd both lost nearly 3½ minutes, the Tour was already moving quickly out of reach.

Because of the intense interest in the looming battle, most observers had little patience for the next three stages. These were won by the opportunist efforts of France's Joel Pelier, Martin Earley of Ireland, and by Belgium's Etienne DeWilde, who outsprinted the entire field around the lake of Bordeaux for his first-ever stage-win in the Tour de France. The race was coming closer to the first mountains, which would bring Delgado an opportunity to show his refound confidence again. The Spaniard dutifully obliged the script-writers by gaining half-a-minute on Fignon, LeMond, Rooks, Theunisse and Kelly at the ski-resort of Cauterets. It was stirring to see two other Spaniards – one from a rival team – act as 'guinea-pigs' for Delgado, especially Miguel Indurain, who'd spent 85 kilometres virtually alone in front, in case Delgado managed to join forces with him. The next day promised even more excitement when, after the descent of the Col du Tourmalet, Delgado sent another team-mate, Julian Gorospe, up the road, before doubling after him a short while later as the race passed through the first feeding station of the day. It was textbook racing, and soon Gorospe was loyally pulling Delgado away from Fignon and LeMond's group at a suicidal – for him – pace. After less than 10 kilometres together, Delgado ordered his team-mate to drop back and try to hinder the others' chase, leaving him to solo majestically up to Mottet and Robert Millar, who had been away together since the start of the Tourmalet climb 40 kilometres earlier. Just 70 kilometres remained ahead, but included in that distance was the obstacle of the Col de Peyresourde and the final climb to Superbagnères – where LeMond had retaliated against Hinault three years earlier.

Such was their combined strengths, and Delgado's motivation, that the trio had a 4½-minute lead as they began the final climb. Fignon's unpopularity amongst his companions, combined with LeMond's lack of climbing strength made the chasers' task even more difficult, for Fignon was left to do most of the work in the 25-strong group, which contained an

Robert Millar was a brilliant winner of the tenth stage to Superbagnères, defeating a highly motivated Pedro Delgado in the summit sprint after the pair – and a tiring Charly Mottet – had taken more than three minutes from Laurent Fignon and Greg LeMond

Majesty incarnate: Laurent Fignon was in superb form throughout the three-weeks racing, and in particular on the Bastille Day stage to Marseille. Here Fignon makes a splendid sight as he enjoys a mid-stage escape with French rival, Charly Mottet. The two Frenchmen were ultimately unable to maintain their acceleration which on several occasions had exceeded 75 kilometres per hour – on the flat!

evergreen Sean Kelly – resplendent in the Green Jersey he was trying to make his own for the fourth time. Ever since Fignon had punched a photographer in the first week of the race, and generally behaved reprehensibly since Luxembourg, nobody seemed too interested in helping him take over the race-lead. This situation undoubtedly kept the leading trio's lead mostly intact as the climb was overcome. But we must give credit where it's due, for not only did the Parisian stick to his task, dragging the best of his group almost all the way to the finishing line – where Millar had outsprinted Delgado for the stage victory nearly 3½ minutes earlier – but in the final push to the summit he actually dislodged the American from his side to take over the Yellow Jersey by just seven seconds.

For the moment all Fignon's troubles seemed to have disappeared – here he was, five years on from his last possession of the fabled jersey, with every reason to believe he could win the Tour one last time. But others weren't so sure: at this stage in the race, and despite Fignon's leadership, it was the amazing Delgado who held most people's attention by the way in which he clawed his way back into contention – quite a turn-around in ten days! LeMond too deserved special attention for what was also a comeback of mega-proportions, but most people predicted the American's surge of exuberance would fizzle out in the high Alps a few days later.

Under a horrendous heatwave, crashes and abandonments provided the interest in the four stages that transferred the race into the Alps for its rest day. The most symbolic victory of the race, so far, went to France's Vincent Barteau, who won the Bastille Day stage into Marseille – a fine prelude to the evening's festivities to celebrate the 200th anniversary of the revolution. A different storming took place on stage 15, when Rooks won the difficult 39-kilometre mountain time-trial to Orcières-Merlette. And this time the favoured synopsis – that Delgado was going to win the Tour again – changed subtly when LeMond rode back into the Yellow Jersey with a magnificent fifth place, just 8 seconds slower than Delgado, but nearly a minute faster than race leader Fignon. Had Delgado used up all his aggression? Had LeMond rediscovered

With Gert-Jan Theunisse way ahead on the stage to L'Alpe d'Huez, LeMond, Fignon and Millar bided their time on the Col de la Croix de Fer, anticipating the ferocity of Delgado's expected attack on the final climb – an attack which never came

his climbing talents? Had Fignon begun, in the last week, the decline his critics were expecting?

All these questions ensured the next stage to Briançon would be a real cracker! It was to take in the damaging climb of the Col de Vars, then the fearsome and legendary Col d'Izoard, where some of the Tour's most epic battles have been fought out. On this climb are sited symbolic memorials to two of the men whose talents helped give the Izoard such a notoriety – Louison Bobet from Brittany and Italy's greatest ever cyclist, Fausto Coppi. Rather sadly, though not surprisingly under the tension that was enveloping the leaders, two lowly placed riders – Swiss champion Pascal Richard and Frenchman Bruno Cornillet – had the honour of being first past the memorials in the mountain's Casse Désert – an eerie moon-like landscape of jutting rock pinnacles and sheer slopes of loose scree. Six minutes after the two fortune-seekers had left the mountain, Delgado accelerated away from the other favourites, showing he still had something to scare LeMond and Fignon with. At the windblown summit, 7,742-feet (2,360 metres) above sea-level, the Spaniard had only Mottet and LeMond for company; and the trio completed one of the most difficult descents in the Tour to arrive in Briançon – and its leg-stinging climb up to the citadel – with a dozen seconds in hand over Fignon. The French rider cracked for the second day in succession on the final climb, just as his group was making contact with LeMond's.

With the toughest stage to come next day, LeMond led Fignon by 53 seconds, a lead which most people felt would be extended on the final climb to L'Alpe d'Huez now that it was Fignon who seemed to be tiring, and not LeMond. But Fignon at least had faith in himself. After the awesomely beautiful climbs of the Col du Galibier and Col de la Croix de Fer, and with Holland's Theunisse already many minutes down the road in his Polka-dot Jersey, the leading contenders entered the cauldron of emotion that 'the Alpe' represents to Tour followers and competitors alike. With everyone expecting Delgado to repeat his 1987 effort here, but with the man himself clearly unable to deliver following his efforts thus far, a

On the lower slopes of the Col de la Croix de Fer, Theunisse is about to make good his escape and begin a superb individual effort to win at L'Alpe d'Huez

A dropped Greg LeMond fights gallantly to restrict his losses at L'Alpe d'Huez, knowing that Fignon has taken over the race lead again

Fignon's attack on the stage to Villard-de-Lans was completely unexpected

Colombian team-mate set a furious pace almost the whole way up the mountain, until with less than 5 kilometres to go, and with tension at breaking-point, Fignon sprang a brutal acceleration away from five rivals: LeMond, Delgado, Rooks, Spain's Marino Lejarreta and Abelardo Rondon the Colombian. Only Delgado had the strength left to respond to this clever attack by the experienced Frenchman – for Fignon was at least as tired as everybody else – and LeMond was the one to crack now, flopping over his handlebars in an effort to maintain his momentum as he had at Superbagnères a week before, though this time the damage was greater by one minute. Now LeMond had lost his hard-won Yellow Jersey by just 26 seconds.

The 'script' for this race had, by now, far exceeded its credibility, such was the magnitude of the racing between LeMond, Delgado and Fignon, and nobody thought it could possibly get any better. But it now seemed likely that Delgado had bravely used up most of his dynamic energy, and the race was down to just two men, for whom victory meant so much. And when one of those men – Fignon – attacked the next day to take a brilliant victory at Villard-de-Lans and increase his lead to an impressive 50 seconds, observers began checking the statistics to see when was the last time a Tour had been decided on its final day. When, at the presentation for the Tour the previous October, a 24·5-kilometre time-trial had been announced as the grand finale for Paris, experienced race followers had predicted a boring, anticlimactic finish to the 1989 Tour – nobody could have possibly predicted the way the

race was heading for its crux, or the speculation and opinion slowly filling everyone's minds as the reality began to dawn upon them. So, too, the same people were exulting in Fignon's return to his glory days of 1983–84, for it had to be said that the blond-haired cyclist was riding in the manner expected of a great Tour winner, a feeling that spread further the following day after Fignon had instigated a brilliant exhibitionist ride by the top five men overall on the five-mountain stage to the lakeside spa resort of Aix-les-Bains. Not to be outdone, however, LeMond jogged the French journalists' confidence of a Fignon victory by easily outsprinting his companions in great style, and with a beaming smile on his face. Fignon too was smiling – yes, even these two were enjoying their racing, and the pleasure it was giving to millions of onlookers worldwide.

The good humour continued next day when, with the mountains finally behind them, the entire peloton let off steam in the first few hours by playing the traditional fools on the final road stage of the race. Some staged a 'mock' crash for the benefit of television, while others showed their individual delight that the Tour was all but over – like Belgium's Michel

The 'famous five' on the road to Aix-les-Bains: Delgado leads from Fignon, Theunisse, Lejarreta and LeMond

Dernies, who swopped his bicycle for an official's £7,000 ($11,000) motorbike and proceeded to overtake an ecstatic crowd of 138 professional cyclists – all that remained of the 198 men who'd set out three weeks before! Even Fignon showed some good morale by agreeing to ride at the front of the bunch for the benefit of photographers wanting their traditional pictures of the Yellow, Green and Polka-dot Jersey winners. But whatever benevolence Fignon might have had then, his antics later that evening after the TGV train ride to Paris decided, once and for all, the 28-year-old's appalling reputation. After a week that had seen even his harshest critics think twice, following his display of strength, intelligence and courage, Fignon duly released a salvo of abuse at a television crew whose 'crime' was to dare film the heir-apparent as he walked away from the train in the Gare du Lyon. Totally unprovoked, the nervous cyclist shoved the cameraman aside, spitting into the lens as he was filming, before ordering the commentator – with some words the producer had to dub over – not to show the footage on screen. The TV station did just that, with the effect that, at prime-time viewing, millions of French people had their evening meals interrupted by this sad display of a Tour de France race leader whose nerves and confidence had been completely shredded.

What LeMond must have made of all this is anybody's guess, but it must have given the now popular American an added boost to see his opponent in the next day's duel behave so erratically. In any case, 99 percent of the Tour's armada of reporters duly did what they habitually do on the eve of the last day – they pre-wrote their final race round-up. In this case they were heralding Fignon's triumphant homecoming in the year the Republic was celebrating its bicentennial. Some provincial journalists even went home on the Saturday evening, preferring to fill in the gaps in their stories from an armchair view of the race – on television! Only a minute handful of exceptionally shrewd, or perhaps blindly loyal, journalists resisted the favoured opinion and sat down in the *Salle de Presse* the next afternoon in front of blank sheets of paper. They were the ones who got away early that evening, able to enjoy the traditional post-race farewell meal, with some of their travelling colleagues, or maybe crack a bottle of champagne to toast the Tour's winner. For the bulk of the reporters, a working stint that would run into the early hours was the penalty for being so certain that Fignon would ride into his home town as the 1989 Tour winner.

The photographers had a heart-stopping last hour as well. The bulk of them – about 60 – were seated on the edge of the pavement at the entry into the Champs Elysées itself, from where they could not only casually shoot off frame after frame of each Tour survivor – sharing a few bottles of wine together in the process – but could gaze across the broad Place de la Concorde to where LeMond could be seen entering the circuit to go around behind the Tuileries Gardens and eventually reappear in the photographers' sights; all too easy, really. Even when the midway time-check had informed everyone that LeMond was 24 seconds ahead, nobody seemed unduly concerned, for Fignon was too experienced to let the race slip from his grasp now – wasn't he? With each rider starting at 2-minute intervals, the photographers were able to see for themselves the time difference after LeMond had been seen speeding onto the circuit – a tiny, ant-like figure surrounded by an unusually massive phalanx of cars and motorbikes, that were themselves completely dwarfed by the grandeur of the French capital. But when more than 2½ minutes had passed, with still no sign of Fignon across the open space, the photographers began to wake up and realize that Fignon could lose this race yet!

Sure enough, LeMond – completely unrecognizable, tucked as he was behind his famous 'tri-bars', and with aerodynamic helmet and dark glasses covering his face – streaked past a clatter of wildly firing camera shutters at over 60 kilometres an hour to begin the long, rising slope to the Arc de Triomphe from where he would drop down again to the finish. It was fifteen seconds short of 3 minutes before Fignon passed the same spot, his plainly shocked face telling its own story. From then on it all happened too quickly. Completing the run to the finishing line at the foot of the

The traditional road stage into Paris was replaced by a time-trial from Versailles in 1989. Nobody could have imagined the suspense that would engulf this normally processional stage

avenue, LeMond skidded to a halt and rode back to the line to await the timekeepers' judgements. Then followed the longest wait of everybody's lives, or so it seemed – and not least LeMond's! The seconds ticked slowly by. . . . Finally, with LeMond holding his head in a mixture of agony, disbelief and expectancy, and refusing to believe the premature cheers of the throng of journalists, photographers and family crowding around him, the announcement was made – as Fignon passed the 100-metres-to-go sign: *'Laurent Fignon a perdu le Tour de France!'*

At this news, LeMond's face lit up with joy. 'You've won Greg! Oh, my God, you've won!' screamed Kathy, his almost hysterical wife, now standing beside the dazzled, victorious rider. Everybody wanted to offer congratulations; media-people who had themselves lived on their nerves for all of three weeks – they all wanted to say their piece, to share in LeMond's earth-shattering achievement, to shout their own whoops of delight into an emotionally charged atmosphere. All of them found it quite impossible to construct a well-framed sentence, or to speak with any degree of eloquence, while television commentators choked on their own silence – it couldn't be possible, surely not! Through all this, the two duellists lived in widely contrasting worlds. LeMond, finally acknowledging he'd won, flung his arms in the air, hugged almost everybody in sight, and then proceeded to tell his story to millions of people around the world through a bizarre cluster of prodding microphones. Fignon at first had been hard to find, mainly because he'd ridden smack into a human wall of reporters and onlookers, and now lay on the ground, wounded more by what his *soigneur* was telling him, than by the impact with the tarmac. Eventually, after several minutes, he managed to compose himself and sat forlornly on an old beer-crate, his head bowed and hidden, his hands covering the tears that flowed so openly, his once golden pony-tail now resembling a sweaty piece of old string. Here, just 50 feet away from the happiest man in the world, was without doubt the saddest sight of the 1989 Tour de France.

He's done it! Greg LeMond at the exact moment he realized he'd won the 1989 Tour de France

151

LAURENT FIGNON:
unrestored glory

Had Laurent Fignon, and not Greg LeMond, won the 1989 Tour, the story of their dog-eat-dog battle would have had a no less staggering conclusion than it in fact achieved; for Fignon's career is even harder to comprehend than that of his American rival. When Fignon emerged as Hinault's logical successor during the 1983 and 1984 Tours de France, the nation's cycling aficionados began licking their lips at the possibility of a future great battle between the two French cyclists. It had been years, in fact decades, since the Tour last had such a treat. Certainly not since the heady days of Jacques Anquetil and Raymond Poulidor had there been any semblance of a real scrap – and their last one had been as far back as 1964, when after some stirring man-to-man battles, Anquetil won the race by a scant 55 seconds.

Being a French race, the Tour never evokes a greater degree of excitement and passion than when two of her own kind are fighting for the lead, and it was for this reason that the next year's race – 1985 – should have been remembered as the one Tour that lived up to the sentiment of that Anquetil–Poulidor epic. But things don't always go the way people might like them to; a damaged Achilles' tendon put Fignon out of the reckoning in 1985, as a result of his over-eagerness in the cold, early-season training races. That was unfortunate enough, but nobody then could have foreseen the troubles that were to dog the next four years of Fignon's life and possibly spoil for ever the career of such a brilliant cyclist. As it was, an expectant public was left to reflect on what might have been, as Hinault eagerly took up France's challenge again.

The previous year Fignon had demonstrated his growing emergence as a future *campionissimo* – a champion of champions – by the way he'd single handedly defeated all-comers to win the 1984 race. In a far more convincing way than in 1983, when Hinault was absent, Fignon proved he had not only the courage and strength required of a future grand champion, but also the mental capacity to withstand the enormous pressure put upon the race leader of a Tour de France. Most importantly, the 23-year-old Parisian proved he

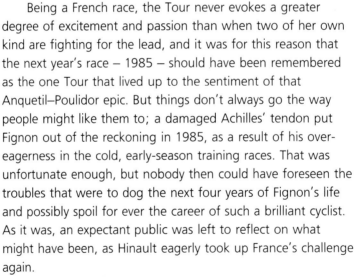

Right: Laurent Fignon hurtles onto the Champs Elysées, his shocked face telling its own story

Left: In 1984 Fignon cut a fine, determined figure with his strange handlebars and hard-shell helmet, as he sped towards the finish of the 67-kilometre test into Le Mans on stage seven – an effort that would put him within reach of his second Tour victory

A youthful Fignon pictured midway through the 1984 Tour . . .

was totally impervious to the intimidation that Hinault so skilfully employed in 1984 – as 'The Badger' always did when his physiological condition was less than perfect.

Fignon won five stages in his 1984 campaign, his Renault-Elf team won the 51-kilometre team time-trial, and additionally he emphatically disposed of Hinault in the crucial L'Alpe d'Huez stage. But what made Fignon's Tour really complete was the fact that he won all three strategic time-trials – Hinault's revered speciality – and then further compounded his rival's jealousy by winning two of the mountain-top finishes, at La Plagne and Crans-Montana. Winning a mountain road race (en-ligne) stage is considered the final proof of a Tour winner's worthiness, and this was something that Hinault at the time had yet to achieve; and consequently it was Hinault who became intimidated this time, succumbing to a final deficit of 10½ minutes in Paris. Because of this, the 1985 Tour de France should have afforded the most memorable battle for decades. But for Fignon at least, it all went wrong.

It's said that one of the unspoken reasons why Hinault, and later, LeMond, left Guimard for La Vie Claire, was that Guimard – a former multi-stage winner in the Tour, who almost won the Green points jersey in 1972 – pushed his young riders too hard. These rumours, and that's all they were, began to re-emerge when Fignon stopped racing at regular intervals at the beginning of the 1985 season, claiming his Achilles tendon was causing him trouble. In the 1985 Tour, with a rejuvenated Hinault on the loose once again, Fignon's absence was conveniently overlooked, but when the bespectacled cyclist failed to materialize for the remainder of the season, the fickle cynics turned up the heat on Fignon, claiming there was more to his injury than mere strained fibres. Surgery had been carried out on his damaged heel, and Fignon stoically explained he would return at the start of the 1986 season, putting the cause of his injuries down to the use of big gears in the earlier part of the year. Whatever people believed – and Fignon made it clear people could believe whatever they wished – the period from June 1985 through to June 1989

... and his 1989 look –
having suffered years of
frustration and ill-health

was rife with stories of ill-health, personal problems, lack of
interest – even drug abuse!

It was not until 12 June 1989 that people began to accept
that Fignon really was on the way back. That humid, sunny day
in Florence, Fignon scored his first-ever victory in the Tour of
Italy – the second most important stage race after the Tour de
France. That he won it with the same degree of courage,
strength and bravado that had last been seen in 1984 seemed
to confirm once and for all his re-emergence as a major force
to be reckoned with. People's attention inevitably turned
towards the Tour de France that was to begin just over two
weeks later: could Fignon possibly win, they asked? The cynics
grew suddenly quiet.

Despite occasional flurries of good form, Fignon had only
finished the Tour de France once since his 1984 victory, and
that was in 1987 when he finished more than eighteen
minutes behind Irishman Stephen Roche in seventh place. A
stage win there – at the same La Plagne where he'd secured
his 1984 Tour victory – was to be the only hint of Fignon's
former greatness in four years of mediocrity in the Tour.

Inconsistency was the real highlight of 1987 — the second year of Fignon's comeback; a fine third place overall in the tough Tour of Spain in May contrasted sharply with last place in the 89-kilometre Grand Prix des Nations time-trial in September — 12 minutes behind his team-mate Charly Mottet! When Fignon hung up his wheels for the year after that débâcle, his 1987 season had proved to be as inconclusive as the previous year's, where a confidence-boosting win in the one-day Flèche-Wallone classic in Belgium was the only triumph. In the Tour — a race on which former winners are inevitably scrutinized — the fading star suffered the humiliation of being dropped by his Système-U team in its winning team time-trial performance. Ironically, Fignon was to retire from the 1986 Tour the night prior to the first mountains in Pau — in the same town and in the same manner as Hinault had done six years earlier.

1988 had begun well enough with a startling win in the opening one-day 'classic' of the season — Milan–San Remo. Good performances followed, to boost Fignon's confidence — though his critics said Fignon's achievements were only gained through opportunism, not strength. Both Fignon and his critics knew this latter commodity would be needed if he were seriously to contest the Tour that summer. Sadly, just when it looked as if the dogged Fignon had got himself back on the rails, fate turned against him — though not for the first time in

A brilliant stage win at La Plagne in 1987 reminded everybody of Fignon's almost forgotten talent

A tapeworm malady brought out the very worst of Fignon's character in the 1988 Tour

his troubled career – when a tapeworm developed in his intestines, a debilitating problem that forced the Parisian to retire in Morzine after the first day in the mountains. It seemed certain that Fignon's dream was finally over, that he'd never be able to overcome this latest setback, and that retirement was inevitable.

As if he didn't have his flagging health to worry about, a galling aggravation lay with his unpopularity amongst the cycling fraternity. With a phlegmatic personality to match that of Hinault, Fignon had never enjoyed much favour with his public, despite the fact that in a few short years Fignon had become the eternal underdog, that symbol of martyrdom that the French in particular are known to adore. In the public's eyes, the studious-looking Parisian couldn't seem to do anything right. When he'd won the Tour in 1983, they'd said it was only because Hinault wasn't there. Then when he beat Hinault the following year, the same public had accused him of ridiculing his 'ageing' rival's efforts. French people seemed happier when Fignon disappeared altogether in 1985; they extolled instead the glorious way in which Hinault had rallied, after crashing and almost losing the race because of his injuries.

1986–87 had been no better, but when Fignon won Milan–San Remo in 1988, his public image at last began to improve. The French began to get behind 'their man', as they belatedly began to appreciate his unstinting efforts to make good once more. But Fignon's disastrous Tour that year ended for good any hope of public goodwill – the sorrowful-looking Fignon would never be a popular sportsman again, a circumstance that ensured his dubious character could only deteriorate. It hadn't gone unnoticed that his incessant struggle against ill-fortune since early 1985 seemed to have taken its toll of Fignon's sanity too; he'd been fined 200 Swiss francs, just a few days before his retirement from the 1988 Tour, for having thrown a full water-bottle at a throng of motorbike photographers crowding around him as he pedalled alongside the race doctor's car. Even though it was obvious that Fignon was reacting to the pressures that living in the public eye can inflict, few people had sympathy for him; and

The youthful smiles that Fignon displayed on the Paris podium in 1984 alongside his proud father, were soon to disappear for ever

that included his own team-mates, who had lost all confidence in Fignon's ability to lead.

Fignon's sensitivity was laid open for all to see from then on; when he'd become France's hero five years earlier, his shaggy blond hair and wire-rimmed Cartier glasses had created an unlikely sporting figure. By the time he began to truly re-emerge in 1988, his golden locks were gathered in a stylish

The saddest sight of the 1989 Tour de France

pony-tail – though cynics mocked that it was only a flamboyant gesture to deflect people's gaze from his receding hairline! Cruel comments maybe, but this touch of vanity seemed to coincide with the start of Fignon's unpredictable behaviour, which was to become a fixed trait during the next two years. During his victorious Tour of Italy, in a build-up to what was meant to be his final resurrection – victory in the 1989 Tour de France – Fignon fought shy of the prying cameras, deliberately turning his face away whenever photographers strayed too close to the troubled star, and on one occasion actually aiming a punch at one of them!

In terms of athleticism, the 1989 Tour went like a dream for Fignon. He had good health, good form, good morale, and showed himself once again to be hungry for the ultimate success. With his typical risk-all manner, he rode his heart out in the Pyrenees to take his first Yellow Jersey since 1984 – and lifted himself to do it again in the Alps after LeMond had grabbed it back in a time-trial. Nobody could deny that Fignon had ridden his heart out the whole way around France; yet still it wasn't enough. In any other year, everything Fignon had done would have been enough to win – and what a win it would have been! But as we now know, 1989 was no ordinary year in the Tour de France and Fignon didn't realize his hopes. Only time will tell whether Fignon ever wins the Tour again, and it has to be said that nobody could really deny him that one last triumph, for Fignon is at the very least a brilliant cyclist, and as such deserves the recognition he strives so hard for. But even by his own demanding levels of perseverance, he may never be able to lift himself as much as he did in 1989. Fate has sometimes a fickle way of dealing out justice, for who is to say whether LeMond's win was more deserving than a Fignon one might have been – for hadn't they both suffered enough? And suppose Fignon had not suffered such bitter fortune when he did – how many Tours might he have won by now? Sadly, what should have been Fignon's greatest victory became, instead, his greatest irony: like Hinault before him, France's troubled cycling star had had his crowning glory taken from him by the same man – Greg LeMond.

INTO THE 21st CENTURY

The eight seconds with which Greg LeMond defeated Fignon in Paris in 1989 is the smallest winning margin in the Tour de France and though nothing can ever again be considered certain after such a see-saw, cliff-hanger of a race, it's unlikely that that tiny margin will ever be reduced in future years. The previous record was set in 1968, when the steady Dutch rider Jan Janssen overcame Herman Van Springel of Belgium by 38 seconds – a gap that must have been considered irreducible then! But LeMond's win, or – depending on how you want to view it – Fignon's defeat, came down to three principal factors: Delgado's 'gift' that afforded so much leeway to two less fit men, the unexpected boost their motivation gleaned from his mistake, and the use of ultra-modern equipment and clothing to reduce wind resistance. The modern professional cyclist, with his sophisticated componentry couldn't be further removed from the image of the pre-First World War Tour de France hero, clad in a variety of rough, baggy, uncomfortable clothing and riding a bike that weighed 10 pounds more than today's light alloy or carbon-fibre machines.

LeMond is the ideal model of what the 21st-century cyclist could be, with his all-American-boy smile, aerodynamically assisted riding style and highly calculated approach to his profession – one that recently saw LeMond become the highest paid cyclist in the history of the sport. Indeed if LeMond hadn't been a professional cyclist for nearly ten years now, he could well be hailed as a prototype of the next century's cycling male. Also, were it not for the unfortunate accident that befell LeMond on a turkey-shoot with some friends in April 1987 – his brother-in-law fired a round of shotgun pellets when he saw movement in a bush that actually hid the champion – we might have been looking to 1990 as the year Greg LeMond sets out to equal his mentor, Bernard Hinault, as a five-times winner of the Tour. But we're not. Instead, we must wait and see if the Californian-born, former freestyle skier, can build on his 1989 reinstatement as potentially the world's top professional and chase more Tour victories; just five weeks after his 1989 Tour victory over Fignon, LeMond scored an astonishing victory in the one-day

Greg LeMond speeds into the Champs Elysées on his way to winning the 1989 Tour de France

World Championship road-race in Chambéry, France, to show the world that the career that had been devastated by the shooting accident was now well and truly back on the rails.

Should LeMond maintain his health and vitality, there's every reason to believe he can fulfil most, if not all, of his potential – he'll become a 29-year-old just a few days before the 1990 Tour begins at Futuroscope – before he reaches retirement age at 32 or 33 years. His exploits at the Chambéry World Championships, following on from his gutsy Tour performance, were proof that not only is he in perfect physical shape again, but more motivated than at any other time in his life, a state of well-being not exactly hindered by his signing a three-year, $5.7 million contract with the French 'Z' team last September! This unprecedented sum of money continues a trend in high salaries for the American: in 1980, when he signed his first contract, he received $50,000 – the highest sum ever paid to a new 'pro'. Then, in 1985, when he joined La Vie Claire, LeMond's advisers secured a three-year contract worth $1 million for the 23-year-old! LeMond does attract one criticism though: it's said that he's more motivated by money than by sheer desire to win. It remains to be seen if achieving a lifetime's security with his latest financial coup reduces LeMond's hunger to win – and thus robs the sport of some potentially superb racing.

The Tour itself has changed its image considerably in the past few years, a change brought about partly by LeMond's involvement, which itself attracted American television into covering this most viewable of sports in a big way. The television giant CBS had already carried film of the 1983 Tour, but expanded its involvement significantly the following year, when LeMond made his début in the race as the reigning World Champion. By 1986, when LeMond won the race, CBS was paying $200,000 for television rights and that sum increased to $1 million per tour when ABC outbid their bitter rivals in the spring of 1988 to clinch the rights for a three-year period, beginning with last year's race. The sheer amount of money generated by the Société du Tour de France has turned the event – the most popular 'live' sporting event in the world

Scenes like this on the Col du Galibier draw millions of television viewers to the Tour

– into a massively commercial entity with tentacles reaching all the way around the world. Fortunately, the Tour de France has managed to retain its glorious athleticism, in spite of monetary influences, in the 10 years that it's taken for it to become a highly profitable enterprise, instead of the subsidized publicity stunt by its publisher-owners – *L'Equipe* and *Le Parisien-Libéré* – that it used to be. The prize money has risen astronomically in the last 10 years too, in accordance with its newer, wealthy image. When Bernard Hinault first won the Tour in 1978, he received just 120,000 francs – a mere pittance compared with what tennis or golf 'stars' could get at the time for less arduous work. When LeMond breezed across the Champs Elysées finishing line in 1989, he'd earned for himself and his Belgian team-mates a £185,000 booty ($300,000) – still way below what Boris Becker earns for winning a two-weeks-long tournament like Wimbledon, or what Seve Ballesteros can expect to take from any of half-a-dozen major golf tournaments, but nevertheless a vast improvement by anyone's standards! Correspondingly, the next few years should bring further parity for cyclists' rewards with other wide-audience sports.

With so much of the world's financial wealth emanating from the United States and Japan, it's inevitable that those countries' 'global' corporations have taken sponsorship

Scenes like this on the Col du Galibier draw millions of television viewers to the Tour

To the outside world, the traditional finish on the Champs Elysées is one of the most symbolic sights of the Tour de France. It's hard to imagine the 'outside world' taking the race away from its homeland

interests in the Tour – Coca-Cola and Toshiba, to name just two – because of the worldwide television audience, which is claimed to be somewhere between 500 million and one billion people!

Internationalization is the keyword when analyzing the Tour's evolution towards the end of the 20th century, and this spreading of wings has further increased the much-vaunted possibility of one day starting the Tour on another continent altogether, with New York, Bogotà – even Tokyo – being considered. To date, the Tour has only once left mainland Europe, and that was in 1974, when, to emphasize the start of a new Channel crossing between Roscoff and Plymouth, the Tour raced for more than four hours up and down a bland-looking dual carriageway in Devon. But that symbolic show of enterprise brought with it cries of derision from the riders and the media, who saw little value in disrupting their already difficult travelling plans further. The fact that HM Customs officers at Exeter airport delayed the Tour entourage's return to French soil by several hours to examine everyone's baggage – even the riders' bicycle frames – sealed the fate of any similar ventures indefinitely! Since then, the race has restricted its excursions to adjoining countries like Holland, Switzerland,

West Germany and Luxembourg, as well as obliging the Belgian nation with frequent visits *en route*.

There had seemed to be a distant chance that North America would host a Tour departure in 1992, with Montreal the beneficiary because of the 350th anniversary of Quebec's founding as a French province. But it's believed that the Société du Tour de France, under the guidance of its newest director, has decided against such a bold move. It's a clear sign that the organizers want to limit the expansion of their race within an acceptable boundary — one which Montreal could fit into, but only because of its heritage. Should the mighty yen or US dollar tempt this very French institution further afield, the Tour de France as we have come to know it will no longer exist. The logistical problems of airlifting 200 cyclists and their support-crews, as well as nearly 2,000 media and organizational personnel, is no longer the obstacle it used to be, with supersonic travel by Concorde available to reduce the discomfort to the riders at least. But the real danger lies in forgetting the Tour's roots; to try flagrantly to exploit its commercial possibilities away from the Gallic culture that the Tour so brazenly flaunts would quickly reduce the race's credibility to that of a circus — and not even the most enterprising of the Tour's directors would want to see that happen. Additionally, a transatlantic start would mean that the Tour's mother country would only get a fortnight's share of the race, which in itself is probably enough to prohibit the possibility of it ever happening.

From the end of the Second World War, the responsibility for organizing the race fell on the shoulders of two men: Jacques Goddet — son of Victor Goddet, a business partner of Henri Desgrange who founded the Tour in 1902 — and Félix Lévitan. The more senior of the two is Goddet, who first directed the race in 1937 and to this day, at the age of 83, is still an active figurehead within the Tour's hierarchy. Lévitan's involvement with the race lasted almost as long — 40 years — but was far more dictatorial than the elder director's grandfatherly approach. Lévitan and Goddet made the perfect couple, with Goddet's respect for tradition perfectly complementing the entrepreneurial talents of Lévitan. Both men also came from a journalistic background, which helped them to project the Tour to the media in a very moderate and realistic way. This aspect of their approach goes a long way to explaining why the Tour has never lost its sheer athletic appeal, despite the scale of the commercialism that has always surrounded it. And it's by no means a coincidence that Jean-Marie Leblanc, the Tour's present race director, is also a highly regarded journalist; for the Tour seems better served with a journalist in charge.

When Lévitan was ousted from his post in the spring of 1987, supposedly because his style had become too autocratic for the Société du Tour de France – but amid rumours of financial discrepancies in the company's then estimated annual turnover of $10 million – the company promoted one of Lévitan's subordinates, a somewhat flamboyant character called Xavier Louy, into the vacant spot, together with a new financial director. Sadly for Louy, and despite the fact that he was an extremely popular man, his stay in office lasted through just two Tours de France – too short a time for the 40-year-old to bring innovations of his own into the Tour, but long enough to show he couldn't command the respect or the resources that a massive enterprise like the Tour de France needs if it is to move with the times. His successor has already shown himself to be a mature, if not shrewd, leader who, backed by sixteen years of cycling journalism, has the support of media and public alike. Leblanc has all the qualities to lead the Tour into the next decade and beyond that towards the 21st century, using both his journalist's knowledge, and the same racing experience which enabled him to finish the Tour de France in 1970 – in 83rd spot nearly 2½ hours behind a certain Eddy Merckx. Yes, Leblanc raced as a professional, for seven years in fact, before turning to journalism.

When news broke of Leblanc's appointment, and that of a new financial director to work with him, experienced Tour followers breathed a huge sigh of relief, for Leblanc is known as a traditionalist, but one very much with an eye on the outside world; he's long been a fervent advocate of the

mondialization of cycling and is actively involved, in a political move to take the sport – not necessarily just the Tour – into a truly worldwide arena. He's also an acknowledged admirer of Greg LeMond, and was one of the few French journalists in 1986 to present LeMond's side of his battle against Hinault. With Leblanc's evident desire to maintain the status quo between traditionalism and expansion, the Tour is in safe hands and can go forward into the next century with the same level of assurance that Lévitan and Goddet gave to the race. And if Greg LeMond proves to be the 'Pied Piper' for the competitors, that won't be so bad either.

LeMond's once resentful mentor, Bernard Hinault, is now a technical director of the Tour de France. He's in as much demand from the French media as he was when he raced in the Tour and is here being filmed during the 1988 Tour from the roof of his official car

TOUR FACTS

The Hinault years

Number of Tour rides: 8
Days in Yellow Jersey: 72
Number of stage victories: 28
Overall victories: 5
Biggest winning margin: 1981 – 14 minutes
34 seconds over Lucien Van Impe of Belgium.
Closest finish: 1985 – 1 minute 42 seconds
over Greg LeMond of the USA.

* Dutchman Joop Zoetemelk rode in and
completed sixteen Tours – a record.

* Eddy Merckx wore the Yellow Jersey 96
times in his seven Tours – a record.

* Eddy Merckx won a total of 35 stages – a
record.

* Eddy Merckx, Jacques Anquetil and Bernard
Hinault have all won five Tours de France – a
record.

On a wing and a prayer

KINGS OF THE MOUNTAINS
1933 Vicente Trueba (Spain)
1934 René Vietto (France)
1935 Felicien Vervaecke (Belgium)
1936 Julian Berrendero (Spain)
1937 Felicien Vervaecke (Belgium)
1938 Gino Bartali (Italy)
1939 Sylvere Maes (Belgium)
1947 Pierre Brambilla (Italy)
1948 Gino Bartali (Italy)
1949 Fausto Coppi (Italy)
1950 Louison Bobet (France)
1951 Raphael Geminiani (France)
1952 Fausto Coppi (Italy)
1953 Jesus Lorono (Spain)
1954 Federico Bahamontes (Spain)
1955 Charly Gaul (Luxembourg)
1956 Charly Gaul (Luxembourg)
1957 Gastone Nencini (Italy)
1958 Federico Bahamontes (Spain)
1959 Federico Bahamontes (Spain)
1960 Imerio Massignan (Italy)
1961 Imerio Massignan (Italy)
1962 Federico Bahamontes (Spain)
1963 Federico Bahamontes (Spain)
1964 Federico Bahamontes (Spain)
1965 Julio Jiminez (Spain)
1966 Julio Jiminez (Spain)
1967 Julio Jiminez (Spain)
1968 Aurelio Gonzalez (Spain)
1969 Eddy Merckx (Belgium)
1970 Eddy Merckx (Belgium)
1971 Lucien Van Impe (Belgium)
1972 Lucien Van Impe (Belgium)
1973 Pedro Torres (Spain)
1974 Dominigo Perurena (Spain)
1975 Lucien Van Impe (Belgium)
1976 Giancarlo Bellini (Italy)
1977 Lucien Van Impe (Belgium)
1978 Mariano Martinez (France)
1979 Giovanni Battaglin (Italy)
1980 Raymond Martin (France)

1981 Lucien Van Impe (Belgium)
1982 Bernard Vallet (France)
1983 Lucien Van Impe (Belgium)
1984 Robert Millar (Scotland)
1985 Luis Herrera (Colombia)
1986 Bernard Hinault (France)
1987 Luis Herrera (Colombia)
1988 Steven Rooks (Holland)
1989 Gert-Jan Theunisse (Holland)

Most overall 'King of the Mountains' victories: Federico Bahamontes (Spain) and Lucien Van Impe (Belgium) with 6 each. Bahamontes in 1954, 1958, 1959, 1962, 1963, 1964 and Van Impe in 1971, 1972, 1975, 1977, 1981, 1983.

* Highest points total: Luis Herrera (Colombia) – 452 in 1987.

* Only six men have won the 'King of the Mountains' award and the Tour de France in the same year: Gino Bartali (Italy) 1938, 1948; Sylvere Maes (Belgium) 1939; Fausto Coppi (Italy) 1952; Federico Bahamontes (Spain) 1959; Eddy Merckx (Belgium) 1969, 1970.

* Highest mountain pass ever used in the Tour de France: Col d'Iseran – 9,088 foot high.

Race for the Green Jersey

POINTS WINNERS
1953 Fritz Schaer (Switzerland)
1954 Ferdi Kubler (Switzerland)
1955 Stan Ockers (Belgium)
1956 Stan Ockers (Belgium)
1957 Jean Forestier (France)
1958 Jean Graczyk (France)
1959 André Darrigade (France)
1960 Jean Graczyk (France)
1961 André Darrigade (France)
1962 Rudi Altig (West Germany)
1963 Rik Van Looy (Belgium)
1964 Jan Janssen (Holland)
1965 Jan Janssen (Holland)
1966 Willy Planckaert (Belgium)
1967 Jan Janssen (Holland)
1968 Franco Bitossi (Italy)
1969 Eddy Merckx (Belgium)
1970 Walter Godefroot (Belgium)
1971 Eddy Merckx (Belgium)
1972 Eddy Merckx (Belgium)
1973 Herman Van Springel (Belgium)
1974 Patrick Sercu (Belgium)
1975 Rik Van Linden (Belgium)
1976 Freddy Maertens (Belgium)
1977 Jacques Esclassan (France)
1978 Freddy Maertens (Belgium)
1979 Bernard Hinault (France)
1980 Rudy Pevenage (Belgium)
1981 Freddy Maertens (Belgium)
1982 Sean Kelly (Ireland)
1983 Sean Kelly (Ireland)
1984 Frank Hoste (Belgium)
1985 Sean Kelly (Ireland)
1986 Eric Vanderaerden (Belgium)
1987 Jean-Paul Van Poppel (Holland)
1988 Eddy Planckaert (Belgium)
1989 Sean Kelly (Ireland)

Most overall points victories: 4 – Sean Kelly (Ireland) 1982, 1983, 1985, 1989.
Highest points total: Sean Kelly (Ireland) – 434 in 1985.

* Eddy Merckx and Bernard Hinault are the only two men to have won both Green and Yellow jerseys in the same Tour – Merckx in 1969, 1971, 1972, Hinault in 1979.

* Freddy Maertens of Belgium shares with Eddy Merckx and Frenchman Charles Pélissier, the record for most stage wins in one Tour – 8 each. Pélissier in 1930, Merckx in 1970 and 1974, Maertens in 1976.

Tour de France winners:

1903 Maurice Garin (France)
1904 Henri Cornet (France)
1905 Louis Troussellier (France)
1906 René Pothier (France)
1907 Lucien Petit-Breton (France)
1908 Lucien Petit-Breton (France)
1909 Francois Faber (Luxembourg)
1910 Octave Lapize (France)
1911 Gustave Garrigou (France)
1912 Odile Defraye (Belgium)
1913 Philipe Thys (Belgium)
1914 Philipe Thys (Belgium)
1919 Firmin Lambot (Belgium)
1920 Philipe Thys (Belgium)
1921 Leon Scieur (Belgium)
1922 Firmin Lambot (Belgium)
1923 Henri Pelissier (France)
1924 Ottavio Bottechia (Italy)
1925 Ottavio Bottechia (Italy)
1926 Lucien Buysse (Belgium)
1927 Nicolas Frantz (Luxembourg)
1928 Nicolas Frantz (Luxembourg)
1929 Maurice Dewaele (Belgium)
1930 André Leducq (France)
1931 Antonin Magne (France)
1932 André Leducq (France)
1933 Georges Speicher (France)
1934 Antonin Magne (France)
1935 Romain Maes (Belgium)
1936 Sylvere Maes (Belgium)
1937 Roger Lapebie (France)
1938 Gino Bartali (italy)
1939 Sylvere Maes (Belgium)
1947 Jean Robic (France)
1948 Gino Bartali (Italy)
1949 Fausto Coppi (Italy)
1950 Ferdinand Kubler (Switzerland)
1951 Hugo Koblet (Switzerland)
1952 Fausto Coppi (Italy)
1953 Louison Bobet (France)
1954 Louison Bobet (France)
1955 Louison Bobet (France)

1956 Roger Walkowiak (France)
1957 Jacques Anquetil (France)
1958 Charly Gaul (Luxembourg)
1959 Federico Bahamontes (Spain)
1960 Gastone Nencini (Italy)
1961 Jacques Anquetil (France)
1962 Jacques Anquetil (France)
1963 Jacques Anquetil (France)
1964 Jacques Anquetil (France)
1965 Felice Gimondi (Italy)
1966 Lucien Aimar (France)
1967 Roger Pingeon (France)
1968 Jan Janssen (Holland)
1969 Eddy Merckx (Belgium)
1970 Eddy Merckx (Belgium)
1971 Eddy Merckx (Belgium)
1972 Eddy Merckx (Belgium)
1973 Luis Ocana (Spain)
1974 Eddy Merckx (Belgium)
1975 Bernard Thevenet (France)
1976 Lucien Van Impe (Belgium)
1977 Bernard Thevenet (France)
1978 Bernard Hinault (France)
1979 Bernard Hinault (France)
1980 Joop Zoetemelk (Holland)
1981 Bernard Hinault (France)
1982 Bernard Hinault (France)
1983 Laurent Fignon (France)
1984 Laurent Fignon (France)
1985 Bernard Hinault (France)
1986 Greg LeMond (USA)
1987 Stephen Roche (Ireland)
1988 Pedro Delgado (Spain)
1989 Greg LeMond (USA)

* Fastest Tour de France ever: 39·142-kilometres-per-hour in 1988.

* Slowest Tour de France ever: 23.96-kilometres-per-hour in 1924.

* Longest Tour de France ever: 5,745 kilometres in 1926.

* Shortest Tour de France ever: 2,428 kilometres in 1903 and 1904.

INDEX

ABC Television, 164
ANC team, the, 125
Agostinho, Joaquim, 27
Aimar, Lucien, 172
Aix-les-Bains, 147
Alcala, Raul, 58ff, 66, 70, 78–79, 121
Alps, the, 15, 27, 63, 65, 70, 95, 106, 128, 161
Alsace, 120
Altig, Rudi, 172
Anderson, Phil, 31, 82, 112
Anquetil, Jacques, 18, 21, 22, 66, 69, 152, 170, 173
Arc de Triomphe, the, 149
Ardennes, the, 138
Auvergne, the, 110
Avignon, 121
Avoriaz, 27, 33, 40, 69, 82, 90

Bagot, Jean Claude, 81
Bahamontes, Frederico, 170, 171, 173
Bartali, Gino, 170, 171, 173
Barteau, Vincent, 142
Bastille Day, 132, 142
Battagrin, Giovanni, 170
Bauer, Steve, 127–128, 131
Bayonne, 18
Bellini, Giancarlo, 66, 170
Bernard, Jean-François, 46–47, 70, 77, 118, 121–122, 126, 127, 131–132
Berrendero, Julian, 170
Besançon, 98
Bitossi, Franco, 172
Blagnac, 121
Bobet, Louison, 21, 69, 144, 170, 173
Bondue, Alain, 85
Bontempi, Guido, 98, 101, 103, 104, 108
Bordeaux, 103, 109, 117, 121, 133, 141
Bottechia, Ottavio, 173
Bouvet, Albert, 82
Brambilla, Pierre, 170
Breu, Beat, 60, 65
Breukink, Eric, 121, 131, 137
Briançon, 144–145
Brittany, 21, 36
Buysse, Lucien, 173

CBS Television, 164
Café de Colombia, 62
Caja Rural team, the, 98
Cassé Désert, the, 144
Castaing, Francis, 109
Cauterets, 115, 141
Chambéry, 164
Champs Elysées, the, 20, 25, 27, 51, 117, 136, 149, 152, 162, 166

Christophe, Eugène, 11, 12, 97
Coca-Cola, 166
Col Bagargui, 60, 62
Col d'Aspin, 132, 141
Col d'Aubisque, 18, 57, 62
Col d'Iseran, 171
Col d'Izoard, 15, 47, 63, 70, 106, 144
Col de Cou, 29
Col de Joux-Plane, 125
Col de Joux-Verte, 65
Col de la Croix de Fer, 72, 74, 144, 145
Col de la République, 8
Col de Luitel, 25
Col de Madelaine, 112, 128
Col de Mente, 132
Col de Peyresourde, 132, 141
Col de Télégraphe, 74
Col de Vars, 144
Col des Saisies, 88
Col du Burdincurutcheta, 54
Col du Galibier, 63, 74, 75, 94, 145, 165
Col du Glandon, 92, 128
Col du Lautaret, 74
Col du Soudet
Col du Tourmalet, 11, 63, 72, 132, 141
Coppi, Fausto, 21, 144, 170, 171, 173
Cornet, Henri, 172
Cornillet, Bruno, 144
Côte de Laffrey, the, 70
Cours Fauriel, the, 42
Crans-Montana, 154
Cubino, Laudelino, 132, 133

Da Salva, Acacio, 138
Darrigade, André, 172
Dauphine Alps, the, 72
De Vos, Henrik, 88
Defraye, Odile, 172
Delgado, Pedro, 42, 46, 60, 70, 74, 77, 78–79, 81, 82, 87, 121, 122, 124–125, 127ff, 162, 173
Dernies, Michel, 148
Desgrange, Henri, 10, 12, 18, 167
Dewaele, Maurice, 173
DeWilde, Etienne, 141
De Wolf, Alphons, 108
Devon, 166
Dijon,125
Dinard, 138
Dominguez, Jorge, 98

Earley, Martin, 141
East Germany, 120
Echave, Frederico, 78–79
Eiffel Tower, the, 13
Elliott, Malcolm. 92, 98, 112, 121, 125

Epinal, 82
Esclassan, Jacques, 172
Evian, 27

Faber, Francois, 172
Faure, 8
Fignon, Laurent, 33–36, 40, 57, 66, 74, 78, 79, 117, 121, 122, 124, 127, 138ff, 152ff, 162, 173
Flanders, 138
Flandria team, the, 110
Flèche-Wallone classic, the, 157
Florence, 155
Fontenay-sous-Bois, 115
Forestier, Jean, 172
France-Inter radio, 35
Frankfurt, 28
Frantz, Nicolas, 173
Fuerte, Anselmo, 78, 124
Futuroscope, 164

Gap, 47, 97
Garin, César, 10
Garin, Maurice, 8, 10, 11, 12, 13, 97, 173
Garrigou, Gustave, 173
Gaul, Charly, 170, 173
Gayant, Martial, 54
Geminiani, Raphael, 90, 170
Gerbi, 8
Gianetti, Maurio, 95
Gimondi, Felice, 173
Giro d'Italia, 11
Goddet, Jacques, 91, 167, 169
    Victor, 167
Godefroot, Walter, 171
Gonzalez, Aurelio, 170
Gorospe, Julian, 141
Graczyk, Jean, 172
'Grand Prix de la Montagne', the, 55ff, 170, 171
Grand Prix des Nations, the, 157
Green Jersey, the, 15, 98ff, 142, 148, 154, 171
    the first, 13
Guimard, Cyrille, 33, 43, 66, 154
Guzet-Neige, 15, 35, 131–132

Haux, Jos, 96
Hampsten, Andy, 46–47, 60, 72, 75, 78, 87, 121
Haughey, Charles, 126
Heiden, Eric, 94
Hermans, Mathieu, 98, 101
Herrera, Luis ('Lucho'), 17, 34, 37, 40, 54, 57, 58, 60–62, 65, 66, 69–70, 72, 77–81, 82, 87, 121, 122, 124, 128, 131, 138, 171
Hinault, Bernard, 12, 13, 15, 18, 21, 22ff, 57, 60, 65, 66, 69, 70, 82 84, 85, 90, 91, 100, 112, 115, 118, 122, 137, 138, 141, 152, 154, 157, 158, 161, 162, 165, 169, 170, 171, 172, 173
Hoste, Frank, 172

Indurain, Miguel, 141

Janssen, Jan, 162, 172, 173
Japan, 165
Jiminez, Julio, 170
'Journal du Tour', 133
Jura, the, 85

KAS team, the, 98
Karlsruhe, 120
Kelly, Sean, 15, 82, 98, 100, 101, 103, 104, 109, 110ff, 121, 127, 131, 141, 142, 172
'King of the Mountains' title, the, see 'Grand Prix de la Montagne', the
Koblet, Hugo, 172
Köechli, Paul, 51
Kubler, Ferdinand, 172, 173
Kuiper, Henie, 27, 28

L'Alpe d'Huez, 25, 27, 34, 35, 48, 57, 63, 72, 74, 75, 77, 78, 81, 104, 108, 112, 122, 124, 127, 131, 144, 145–146, 154
L'Auto, see L'Equipe
L'Equipe, 8, 12, 165
La Plagne, 87, 124, 154, 155, 157
La Redoute team, the, 82, 85, 90
La Vie Claire team, the, 33, 36, 44, 51, 154, 164
Lambot, Firmin, 173
Lapebie, Roger, 173
Lapize, Octave, 18, 172
Laplume, 28
Larmont hill, the, 90
Lauritzen, Dag-Otto, 87, 121
Le Guilloux, Maurice, 51
Le Mans, 152
Le Parisien-Libéré, 165
Leali, Bruno, 92
Leblanc, Jean-Marie, 137, 168–169
Leducq, André, 173
Lefèvre, Géo, 8
Leiden, 25
Lejarrela, Marino, 70, 77, 78, 110, 146, 147
LeMond, Greg, 20–21, 34, 37, 39, 40ff, 70, 74, 82, 115, 118, 127, 137ff, 152, 154, 161, 162–165, 169, 170, 173
    Kathy, 151

Lévitan, Felix, 167–168, 169
Liège-Bastogne-Liège classic, the, 6
Lievin, 132
Lille, 28
London, 166
Loos, Ludo, 65
Lorono, Jesus, 170
Louy, Xavier, 62, 133, 137, 168
Luxembourg, 167
    prologue, the, 115, 137, 138, 142
Luz-Ardiden, 40, 42, 62, 63, 79, 81, 87, 121, 132, 133
Lyon, 8

Maertens, Freddy, 110, 112, 115, 172
Maes, Romain, 173
Maes, Sylvere, 170, 171, 173
Magne, Antonin, 172
Marseille, 8, 142
Martin, Raymond, 28, 65, 170
Martinez, Mariano, 170
Massif Central, the, 108
Massignan, Imerio, 170
Matthijs, Rudy, 115
Memories of the Peloton, 45
Merckx, Eddy, 6, 7, 18, 21, 22, 25, 29, 51, 53, 66, 69, 100, 115, 126, 168, 170, 171, 172, 173
Metz, 25
Mexico City, 6
Milan-San Remo classic, the, 6, 157, 158
Millar, Robert, 35, 60, 70, 121, 132, 141, 142, 144, 171
Mont Ventoux, 91, 118, 121
Montpellier, 96
Montreal, 167
Morzine, 40, 65, 90, 125, 127, 128, 158
Mottet, Charly, 77, 121, 122, 131, 141, 142, 144, 157

Nancy, 25, 110
Nantes time-trial, the, 10, 45, 106
Nencini, Gastone, 170, 173
Nevada desert, the, 43
New York, 166
Nice, 29
Nive valley, the, 54

Ocana, Luis, 172
Ockers, Stan, 172
Orcières-Merlette, 115, 142

PDM team, the, 115, 131
Parc des Princes stadium, the, 10
Paris, 10, 13, 25, 31, 43, 45, 62, 77, 88, 115, 126, 128, 146, 148, 149, 154, 159
Paris-Roubaix classic, the, 6, 10, 11
Parra, Fabio, 79, 81, 87, 124, 127, 128, 131, 138
Pas de Morgins, 37
Pau, 31, 42, 46, 62, 112, 121, 157
Pedersen, Jørgen, 82, 85, 90
Peeters, Ludo, 65
Pelier, Joel, 141
Pélissier, Charles, 172
Pélissier, Henri, 173
Perurena, Domingo, 170
Petit-Breton, Lucien, 21, 172
Pevenage, Rudy, 172
Peyresourde Pass, the, 46
Phinney, Davis, 121
Piasecki, Lech, 118
Pingeon, Roger, 172
Planckaert, Eddy, 98, 106, 108, 171
Planckaert, Willy, 172
Plumelec, 36
Plymouth, 166
Poitiers, 110
Polka-dot Jersey, the, 15, 40, 54, 60, 62, 65, 69, 70, 72, 77, 78, 98, 131, 145, 148
Pollentier, Michel, 25–26
Pontarlier, 82, 85, 90
Porte, Gérard, 82
Pothier, René, 10, 173
Poulidor, Raymond, 66, 152
Probenicid, 136
Prologue, the (Tour de France), 18, 28, 29, 34, 36, 45, 137
Promenade des Anglais, 29
Puy de Dôme, the, 43, 44, 51, 108, 117, 133, 134, 136
Pyrenees, the, 12, 15, 18, 39, 42, 54, 57, 58, 60, 63, 65, 70, 72, 95, 104–106, 121, 132, 161

Raleigh, 29
    team, the, 37
Ramirez, Martin, 88
Renault-Elf team, the, 154
Renault-Gitane team, the, 28
Rennes, 115
Reynolds team, the, 138
Rheims, 109
Rhône valley, the, 8

Richard, Pascal, 144
Robic, Jean, 172
Roche, Stephen, 37, 60, 70, 77, 78, 81, 87, 118ff, 127, 141, 155, 173
    Lydia, 126
Romanche valley, the, 74, 78, 131
Rondon, Abelardo, 146
Rooks, Steven, 15, 37, 54, 72, 77, 128, 131, 132, 133, 137, 141, 142, 146, 171
Roscoff, 166
Roubaix, 27

St Etienne, 12, 25, 28, 40, 51, 90, 110
St. Marie de Campan, 12
Saint Priest, 31
Sallanches, 29
Savoie Alps, the, 40, 69
Schaer, Fritz, 172
Scieur, Leon, 172
Sercu, Patrick, 172
Sherwen, Paul, 82–85, 90–91
Simon, Pascal, 90–91
Simon, Regis, 85
Simpson, Tom, 91, 121
Société du Tour de France, the, 137, 164, 167, 168
Speicher, Georges, 173
Strasbourg, 37
Superbagnères, 46, 51, 74, 94, 108, 141, 146
Superconfex team, the, 98
Switzerland, 37, 167
Système-U team, the, 122, 157

Tapie, Bernard, 37
Teka team, the, 125
'The Badger', see Hinault, Bernard
Theunisse, Gert Jan, 72, 74, 77, 81, 131, 134, 141, 144, 145, 147, 171
Thevenet, Bernard, 22, 173
Thonon-les-Bains, 29
Thys, Philipe, 173
Tokyo, 166
Torres, Pedro, 170
Toshiba, 166
Tour de France and Its Heroes, 21
Tour de L'Avenir, 43
Tour of Flanders, the, 6
Tour of Italy, the, 6, 26, 28, 78, 125, 126, 155, 161
Tour of Spain, the, 6, 33, 78, 110, 112, 137, 157
Tourmalet Pass, the, 42, 46

'tri-bars', 149
Troussellier, Louis, 173
Trueba, Vicente, 170

Union Cycliste Internationale (UCI), 127
United States, the, 165, 167

Vallet, Bernard, 65, 171
Van Impe, Lucien, 28, 29, 31, 65, 66, 69, 72, 77, 81, 170, 171, 173
Van Linden, Rik, 172
Van Looy, Rik, 172
Van Poppel, Jean-Paul, 98, 100, 103, 108, 120–121, 133, 172
Van Springel, Herman, 162, 172
Van Vliet, Teun, 127
Vanderaerden, Eric, 37, 98, 101, 103, 104, 106, 108, 109, 110, 115, 172
Vaucluse, the, 121
Verney reservoir, the, 74
Versailles, 149
Vervaecke, Felicien, 170
Vietto, René, 170
Villach (Austria), 126
Villard-de-Lans, 40, 77, 122, 131, 133, 146
Villefranche, 117
Villers-sur-Mer, 101
Vitre, 115
Vosges, the, 60
Vuelta à España, 11, 78

Walkowiak, Roger, 172
Wasquehal, 96, 127
West Germany, 118, 167
    West Berlin, 118
Wijnands, Ad, 84
Winnen, Peter, 65
World Championships, the, 29, 33, 126, 164

Yates, Sean, 96, 127
Yellow Jersey, the, 25, 26, 27, 28, 31, 40, 42, 47, 48, 53, 54, 57, 65, 66, 81, 90, 97, 100, 104, 112, 115, 118, 121, 122, 125, 127, 131, 132, 138, 142, 148, 161, 170, 171
    the first, 12

'Z' team, the, 164
Zimmerman, Urs, 47, 48, 131
Zoetemelk, Joop, 25, 27, 28, 29, 51, 112, 170, 173